ZERO

INVESTMENT

BUSINESS

60 MINUTES GUIDE TO
6 FIGURE CAREER IN DESIGN

ZERO
INVESTMENT
BUSINESS

60 MINUTES GUIDE TO 6 FIGURE CAREER IN DESIGN

written by

AR. SOMALI G SINHA

ADHYYAN BOOKS

Zero Investment Business

1st Edition

Publication Date: February 2020
Price: ₹399 | $ 16.00
ISBN: 978-93-88644-60-0

Published by:
Adhyyan Books
Office No. 637,
Opposite Vivanta by Taj,
DDA SFS. Pocket-1, Dwarka,
Sec-22, New Delhi-110077
Website: http://adhyyanbooks.com
E-mail: contact@adhyyanbooks.com

Acknowledgement

Whatever I do in my small world is inspired by my mom. I would also like to mention my father and my husband for supporting me in everything I do. I never ignore contribution of all my mentors and business gurus from whomever I have learnt anything related to Interior Design business. I am thankful to them for empowering and helping me to walk the journey of an entrepreneur. Mr. Bibhash Nag Chowdhry, Mr. Daljit Singh Bhatia, Mr. Debashish Dasgupta (Delhi), Mr. Rafigul Islam (Dhaka). Last but not least, my final inspiration is my Ten-year-old son and Twenty-year-old daughter.

About The Book!

Hi! This is Architect Somali. I am glad to see that you have taken up the challenge of becoming an entrepreneur in the field of Design that you are passionate about. Most of the people who are creative say that they are not a very good business owner. The record shows people who are creative and artistic are introvert. On the other hand, extrovert people are good salesmen and can sell anything and everything to become a successful business owner. My book is all about them who are either strong at the right brain activity that is creativity but not strong at the left brain activity that is mathematics, calculations, science, technology or communication or just the opposite. I know you are surprised to know this.

By following the step-by-step method, you are going to balance both whether you are a school student, college champs, a housewife, a family business owner or the one who has already done some design courses or having some idea. This step-by-step method is going to empower you with the confidence that is required to become an entrepreneur. In most of the cases, in spite of completing technical courses on design, we do not find ourselves fit for business, employment or self- employment. Because there is always a gap between the bookish knowledge and the actual mechanism. For some simple things like methodically approaching a specific problem, presenting ideas properly and starting from scratch to the end of the project with details, we usually forget to make our design sellable. This is where this book will help you overcome the gap apart from sharing the best practices.

You have purchased this book to become an entrepreneur! And I am sure you can do it.

This book will show you how!

I believe that people are what they are today because of their own choices. So, since you have chosen this volume of the series, you will surely be able to start your own business by the end of this book and most importantly; without any investment!

Yes, I mean it!

Let me share with you that for any business to succeed, you need to do lots of hard work; rather you need to do SMART WORK nowadays. Gone are the days where one had to study a lot to get a degree, then work a lot to gain experience and then sacrifice a lot to become successful. In today's scenario, it's irrelevant. You need to Observe, Listen, Learn and Apply continuously.

Search and create smart work to make it sellable. Get recognition, be visible in the market and succeed. I will help you achieve all these in small simple steps so that you can jump-start and get a breakthrough.

Each chapter has tips, notes, figures and exercises to make it easy to follow. So, are you ready?

Let's begin!!!

About The Author!

Ar. SOMALI G SINHA

Director, PROFEX ITE

Ms. Somali Sinha is an Architect who is the director and owner of multiple creative and CAD Skill, Creative Design Skill & Project Planning and Management Skill Development Institution in Bengal. She empowers the jobseeker youth to become employable or entrepreneur in the field of Engineering CAD, Management and Design especially Fashion, Interior & Architecture, Jewelry, Graphics, Web and Animation.

Somali completed her Bachelor of Architecture in 1997 from IIEST, Shibpur, formerly known as Bengal Engineering College. Thereafter, she worked in the Architecture and Building industry for 10 years in various National and International spaces like Bangladesh, Nepal, UAE. She is also an MBA in Project Planning and Management and ITA certified trainer in MS Project.

Being a powerful woman entrepreneur, she started her own training centre in 2007 on a 230 sq.ft space with a single computer. Thereon, she collaborated with the globally largest CAD-CAM training centre as a franchisee partner, to train the engineers on design software. Later she extended the training to people from all backgrounds who are keen and talented in the field of creative design. Presently, she runs 3 campuses in Kolkata ParkStreet with 7000 + sq.ft. area. She has trained over 2000+ Engineers and 1000+ Designers with a thriving ratio of successful placement and self- employment.

As a winner and mentor for students, she has won various national awards since a decade. Some of her accolades include the Highest Collection Award CADD Centre East 2008-09, Highest Growth Award CADD Centre 2010-11, Excellence in Business Growth 2011-12, Optimum Course Material Usage Award 2012-13, Top Contributor Award, LightZap Design Contest DreamZone 2013-14, Best Presentation Award in multifunctional Space Design 2014-15, ABID Architectural Design award-2016, Active Participation in National Events Award 2016-17, Special Jury Awards Interior Trends 2017, Miss India Khadi, Kolkata, Best Dress Designer Award-2018, Participation as Model, Volunteer and Designer on achieving the Unique World Record for the Longest Fashion show, Vibes 360 & Brand Runway December 2018.

She is also a member of the Indian Institute of Architects and Council of Architecture. In regards to her concern for Calcutta, she acted as one of the delegates from various chambers in the education sector to promote Indian design studies in the International market place. Since the last 11 years, she has completely devoted herself to educating and skilling the youth by unleashing their creativity through proper training.

Being the Founder Director of PROFEX Group of Skill Development Institution, she has imparted various Motivational mind trainings to Schools, Colleges and Corporates, "Success Gyan", "Passion to Profession", "Jumpstart and Break Through", "Employability Skill Development" series, to name a few. She is the mastermind of "EnTEENpreneur EXPO", a platform to encourage creative bend of mind of teenage entrepreneurs, a 3-day exhibition space for creative and performing Arts, running for consecutive 3 years in ICCR, Kolkata, "ARTISAN"- Drawing competition in the field of Interior, Fashion, Jewelry, Photography, Graphics & Animation- A Khoj for Artistic minds, running successfully for last 5 years among schools and colleges. She has acted as the jury member for different Architectural, Design competitions, Fashion shows like Khadi Miss India 2017, Kolkata couture 2018, Mr. & Miss India 2019, Kolkata Audition, to name a few.

Presently, with complete responsibility for academic and administrative decision-making, she is successfully practicing the entire strategic planning for Business Development, Branding, Marketing in digital, Social, Print media and BTL promotions. She is committed to accord quality education, Creative Skills & Employability to the youth, working towards a sustainable global quality education that is in alignment with the ecosystem.

Currently she is working in a mission of empowering 10000 creative minds to become either entepprenure or employable.

Content!

Ten Simple Steps To Earn Millions From Your Creativity And Passion.

Step 1:- Be passionate about what you do. Know the elements and use them. Organize them correctly. Apply design principles that are one or more than one in number. Apply Color, Texture and Light. It's all about mind and human psychology. Do some freehand graphics and composition. Now you have started loving the subject. It is now time to test your ability and passion.

Step 2:- Inspiration comes from Nature. Observe, Note, And Apply. Know the process of creating a concept by engineering inspiration boards and mood boards. Benchmarking helps to maintain quality. Awareness of copyrights is necessary. Differentiate to bring uniqueness into your design.

Add your signature style to it.

Step 3:- Be Technical, Touch of Engineering: By using graphs you can easily learn a bit of technical drawing and can understand the relation between various types of drafting. It helps to present your thought appropriately and detailing the same for execution without any deviation and with maximum accuracy.

Step 4:- Our brain thinks in 3D elevation. This is the best way to present your ideas for non- technical clients. Learn to draw the perspective without much engineering. Learn to add some depth in your presentation by adding shades and shadows. Be conversant with sketching One-point and Two-point perspectives before you take the help of any 3Dimensional software.

Step 5:- Be Decisive-Design Decision Process

This step needs to be practiced parallel to the next step. To do effective space planning, you need to plan. So, plan your activity before you start. Know how to plot those Activities in Design charts. Zoning (Macro & Micro) helps in organizing the spaces with functionality; Weightage helps to reach the finest possibilities of space utilization.

While finalizing, consider Life of Design (Design Durability), Level of Comfort (Anthropometry), Sustainability & in some cases Science vs. Belief like Vastu, Feng Shui, etc.

Step 6:- Go by Strategy and Be Methodical

This step needs to be practiced parallel to the previous step. Prepare a standard questionnaire with all the possible questions for your clients to know their needs, wants and desires. Analyze and synthesize the data collected from various sources. Compare alternative thoughts and give weightage to reach the finest one. Reach the best solution.

Step 7:- Be "Material"-istic (Knowledge of Materials)

Before you proceed with the detailing, it is essential to

have complete awareness of the materials and their market price. Knowledge of availability and application of traditional and new materials are also important here. Awareness of the areas of application on different Interior elements like floor, wall, ceiling, etc. in a traditional and non-traditional way will be addressed here.

Step 8:- Be Professional

Before you get into any project, you need to consider all the legal aspects, business ethics, probable remuneration, different types of contracts and understanding in practice, By-Laws, etc. Here I will also elaborate on how to do the project budgeting, the difference between Budget or Rough or Preliminary estimate, Specification, Bill of Quantities and Claim process.

Step 9:- Manage your Project

Knowing the probable constraints beforehand helps to face the same and take remedial steps. So, it is very important to know how to handle Scope, Time, Cost and the Triple-constraint. To overcome these it's very important to be resourceful and knowledgeable. There are 10 different knowledge areas where constant monitoring helps in the successful completion of a project. Here, I will shine the torch on all of them with more emphasis on the ones that are more important.

Step 10:- Successful sales lead to Abundance

Knowing how to do successful sales is important all through

the project process. To maintain balance throughout, you require to balance all the aspects of your life and some interpersonal skills are also required also required 'to manage clients effectively for business abundance'.

Automation is required for Lead generation and CRM helps build References. This is what results in an abundance of the number of projects, thereby, empowering you to earn in millions by transforming your creativity into your passion and your passion into your profession.

After you go through every single topic covered here, in spite of being a non-technical guy from a non- engineering background, irrespective of Science, Arts or Commerce background, you will be able to become a successful entrepreneur in the field of creative design.

So, let's begin the journey with the first step.

STEP 1

Be Passionate (Passion to profession)

I have sub-titled this chapter as passion to profession because of a specific reason that you would know are you continue to read further.

Most of us are not very sure about our career, we are guided by either our parents, friends or visual aids like marketing communication. We see something on the television, mobile or internet and we want to be like that but let me make it clear to you; that may not be our passion all the time. And if it is not your passion, you are most likely going to fail in this business. So, let me help you in unearthing your passion first. I will guide you through the steps on how you can find out what exactly you are passionate about. As here we are discussing about

Design, especially, Interior design and related fields, so let us concentrate on our passion related to design.

While attending a lecture during your school or college days have you ever knowingly or unknowingly started sketching on your rough copy instead of concentrating on that particular lecture, if yes then you are Sketching Freak and passionate about drawing. During your childhood, if you have got a very good Smiley from your science teacher on your science diagrams without knowing that it is not going to give you a career in design then you are a drawing Master. When you enter somebody's house, do you notice if something is not matching, if something is not kept in a manner which it is supposed to be, something looks very odd or something looks very nice, then that is your observation skill. If you inherit a few skills like Sketching, Drawing, Observing, Matching, Arranging things nicely, etc., you are talented. We find our talent from our day-to-day activities only. You can also identify your passion.

Still, if you are a bit confused about your passion, there is a foolproof method of testing your talent, ability and passion about design. Once you finish reading this paragraph, don't miss to take the test. If you score more than 50%, you will be able to complete all the upcoming steps in this book, you can become a successful designer and start earning in 6 figures. Here is the link for you.

http://www.testmycreativity.com/

A sample done

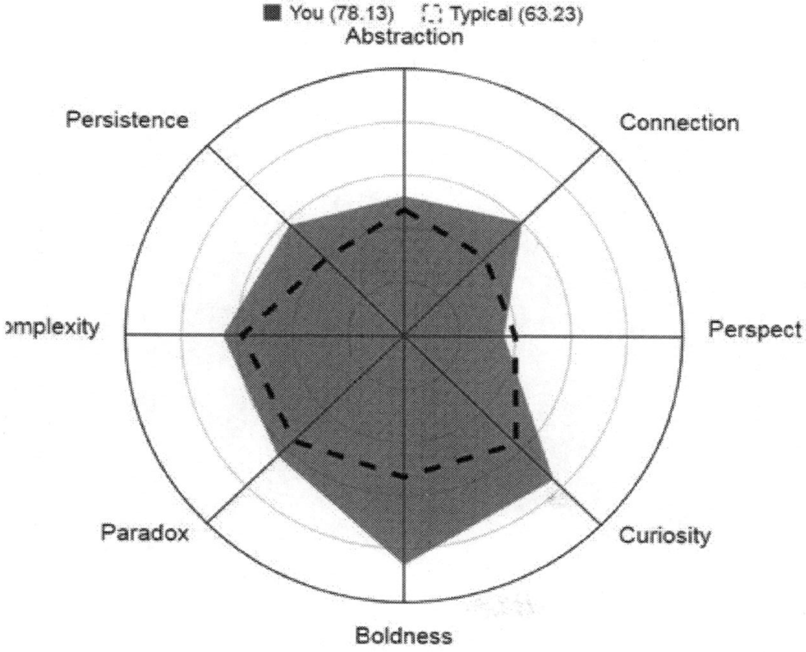

Abstraction The ability to abstract concepts from ideas

Connection The ability to make connections between things that don't initially have an apparent connection

Perspective The ability to shift ones perspective on a situation - in terms of space and time, and other people

Curiosity The desire to change or improve things that everyone else accepts as the norm

Boldness The confidence to push boundaries beyond accepted conventions. Also the ability to eliminate fear of what others think of you

Paradox The ability to simultaneously accept and work with statements that are contradictory

Complexity The ability to carry large quantities of information and be able to manipulate and manage the relationships between such information

Persistence The ability to force oneself to keep trying to derive more and stronger solutions even when good ones have already been generated

Now since you have identified your passion for design and drawing, now you need to reinforce your passion to be always passionate about what you are doing. Success is something that can eventuate in any profession if you are passionate about that. Usually, most of us get inspired by another person's fast-paced success and we try to be passionate about the same profession. However, I will suggest you to do this the other way round. Once you are passionate about design and you are very much sure that yes this is your inner calling or this is the subject that you like most then getting inspired is not very difficult. In the next chapter, I will share more about inspiration. But first, you have to be passionate about Design. When you are passionate, it will help you immensely to understand the subject from the very basics and fundamentals. I have tried to cover the significant facts related to the fundamentals of design here.

Know Eight basic Design Elements first!

While you are designing passionately, you have to remember two things; in this world, nothing happens automatically or it is so designed to follow a certain set of rules what we call design principle. Design principles are applied to certain design elements, so you need to know about design elements and design principles both.

The eight design elements are Point, Line, Plane, Shapes, Volume/Mass, Color, Texture and Light.

Point is having a no dimension.

Line: By adding more points or dots we get a line. Or by joining two points we get a line. So Line is having its length or dimension. There are various ways to create a line. A line can be a continuous line by joining the dots without any gap as that becomes a continuous line. If we place the dots with gaps in between that becomes a dotted line. A longer dash at an interval creates a dashed line or hidden line. These lines are used to show the hidden things in our drawing, I will explain more on this in the Technical drawing chapter. We can create new types of lines by getting inspiration from nature or surroundings. Even if we are writing some letters like A b c d all these are transformation from the line only. Continuous lines with different thicknesses are also in practice. A bold line is used to show the object which is close or the main subject and a thin line is used to project the object which is far away.

Now **plane**. Plane can be created by moving one continuous line towards another direction or by sketching multiple lines side by side. Some examples of a plane are floor or ceiling. Floor and ceiling are horizontal planes while the walls are on the vertical planes.

Shapes can be defined in three ways. First, we get our inspiration from the Nature where natural shapes are available in plenty. Like the shape of a maple leaf, the shape of a river or a mountain, all these are unique every time.

These are called **Natural shape**. The second type of Shape is the geometrical shape. **Geometrical shapes** are of two types; two dimensional and three dimensional. We have studied this in the school-level geometry. Two-dimensional shapes start with a Triangle (3 sides) square rectangle trapezium (4 sides), pentagon (5), hexagon (6), Octagon (8) and depend upon the number of sizes like the various polygons, circles and ellipses. Now let us add a third dimension (z) or height to all these two-dimensional shapes, it then becomes 3-dimensional shapes. Like a circle with a pointed tip becomes a cone, circle with another circle connected to each other becomes cylinder, triangle and square, they can have their third dimension to make a Prism or Pyramid, etc. The third type of shape is the man-made shape. You can create as many as possible and as differently as possible.

Geometrical shapes are those like triangle, square, rectangle, rhombus, rhomboid, trapezium, circle, ellipse, pentagon, hexagon, octagon, etc. Geometrical shapes can have a third dimension too like prisms and pyramids with different types of 2D geometrical bases.

We can also create our own shapes. Creating new shapes reflects on graphic representations.

Volume: - Move a plane towards the third dimension. In terms of length, breadth and height, it becomes three-dimensional. E.g. dice. Massing is the process of playing with volume. The depth of your design increases with more and more arrangements of masses.

Everything beautiful in this world is a marvelous COMPOSITION. Whatever we see around us, that looks good or beautiful, are those which follows certain design principle and has been created by using some design elements. The things around us that do not look good to our eyes or mind are actually not bad designs, rather they are the designs that do not meet the basic design principles. So be cautious when creating something new.

Apply elements on a blank canvas. Try this exercise on a blank wall or a white paper. You have the following elements to apply on it. Let us summarize all the elements.

Color: Color does not exist in real life. It is just the effect of electromagnetic waves registered by our brain and eyes. Yet, it plays a very important role and we simply canot imagine life without it. Color creates feelings and moods and it owes to these features that designers and homeowners need to utilize it wisely in order to create an appropriate atmosphere in a given space. In this guide, we will study the psychological effects of color on the human mind and also the tips to use color in interior design theory.

Understanding psychological effects of color in Interior Design:

Color is an element of light. Different colors create different moods in your home by communicating diverse feelings such as excitement, passion, serenity or mystery. By understanding color theory in interior design, you can create just the right mood you are looking for. It is important to note that each color has a different impact on different people. Many factors can influence these including one‘s age, race, culture as well as life experiences. However, people always respond to color - no matter what. In general, the following colors create the following psychological effects in the home:

1. Psychological effects of color red in the home

Red is the color of fire, passion, danger and strength. This bold color stimulates and excites. It can be warm and inviting and can also make you feel energetic. Avoid using too much red as it can be over-stimulating in the home.

2. Psychological effects of Orange

People who love red but they are not too fond of its aggressive impact so you can replace it safely with orange. This fun, energetic color is ideal for kid‘s room, dining room, office, and even the living room. It symbolizes courage and hospitality. It also makes you feel energetic, adventurous and friendly.

3. Psychological effects of Yellow

According to the color psychology in interior design, yellow is the color of warmth, wisdom, prosperity, sympathy and cowardice. A room colored in yellow can look cheerful, friendly and airy. Avoid using it in large amounts as it can be overstimulating.

4. Psychological effects of Blue

Blue is an important color in interior design theory and it affects the human mind profoundly. There is a reason why blue is the perfect color for bedrooms. It instills a sense of serenity and peace and can be a very soothing color. In bathrooms, it can be used for creating a spa-like tranquil atmosphere. This cool, quiet and reserved color can also represent formality. It is best when paired with white or other lighter hues. Too much of blue can be depressing, so use it wisely.

5. Psychological effects of Green

Green, as we very well know, is the color of nature. It also symbolizes hope, good luck and abundance. It is a cool and friendly color that mixes well with many other colors. It looks great with white and can be used in living rooms, bedrooms and offices.

6. Psychological effects of purple

Purple works very well with other colors. You can pair it up with other jewel tones like emerald green or even with light complementary hues like beige, yellow or baby pink. It is an ideal color in girl‘s rooms. The psychological effects of purple in the homework to give the space a dignified and dramatic look. Purple, after all, is the color of royalty.

7. Psychological effects of black

Black is associated with evil, mourning and death. However, it is also the color of wisdom. Black, in interior design theory, is always used in small amounts with contrasting, complementary colors.

When used right, it can add depth and timeless elegance to a room. Avoid using black in large quantities as it can seem oppressive.

8. Psychological effects of white

This fresh, peaceful color is used widely in interior design theory where it can instill feelings of youthfulness, faith and innocence. White can help smaller spaces appear large. It can also make rooms look livelier, fresher and crisper.

Choosing interior design colors based on their psychological impacts

It is clear that people tend to feel comfortable with the colors that reflect their personalities. For example, a bold, passionate person might feel happier in a red or orange-colored room. However, a shy person may not feel comfortable in a red room but might feel better in rooms with soft blue or light green shades. The best thing interior designers can do when selecting colors for their client's homes is, they can use their preferences in individual sleeping areas and select those colors in common areas such as the living room and kitchen. This can make all the members feel as comfortable as possible. No single choice will satisfy everyone but one must attempt to use those colors which help match the goals of all individuals. I hope this guide helps you select your paint colors easily.

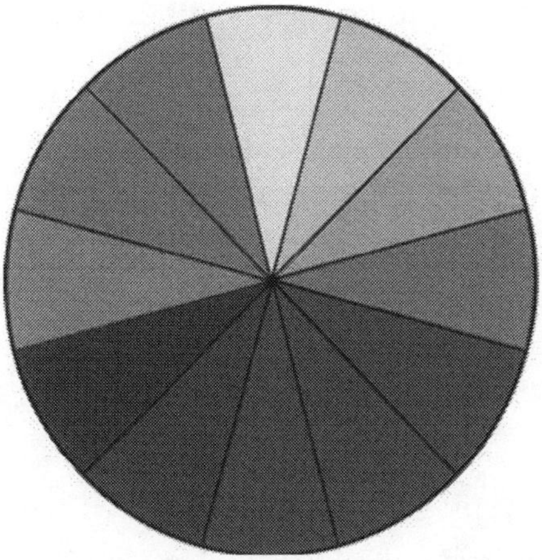

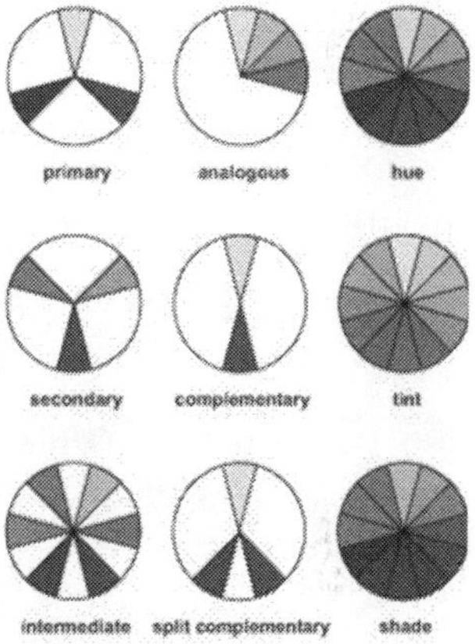

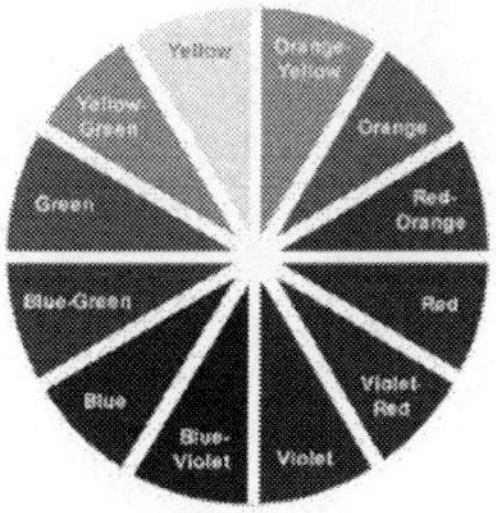

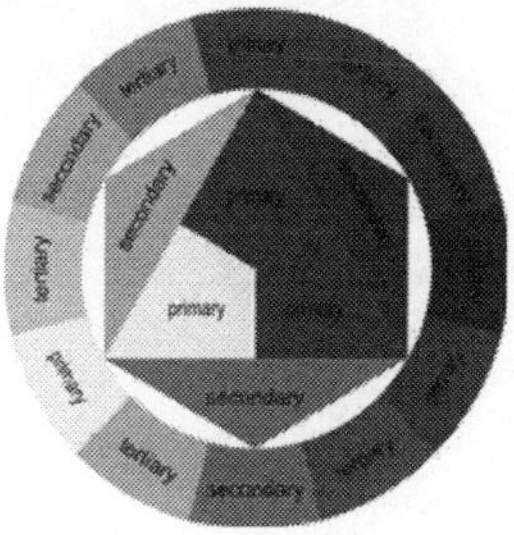

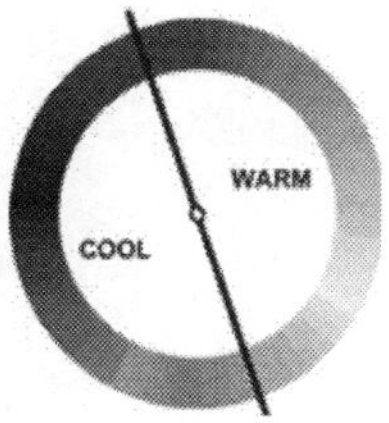

Texture:

What Do We Mean By "Texture"?

This is a good question that I am usually asked in my coaching sessions. In design parlance, it is often defined as "the sensations caused by the external surface of objects received through the sense of touch". It is basically about how things feel. Think about squishing the soft carpet between your toes, running your hand along a rough wooden tabletop, or sinking down into leather couch cushions.

Honestly, we think that the "sense of touch" part of the definition should be revised to say "perceived" sense of touch. Anyone who has ever watched an interior design TV program or flipped through the pages of a magazine can tell you that you don't need to have physical contact with a room to feel the power of texture.

While the texture may play a supporting role in the function of the space, it is no less vital to a design's success. Instead of the examples of texture above, imagine yourself trying to get comfortable on a seating set made of granite. Always consider how the texture will elevate the overall experience of your design.

Texture Adds Visual Weight

Visual weight is something that your brain can feel without even touching the surface. Remember when we talked about color theory, we discussed how using a warm or cool color can affect how the space feels. Texture works in a similar way. Rough textures are more likely to make a space feel intimate and grounded while smooth textures bring a sleeker more aloof tone to the room.

You should also consider the placement of textures as you go about designing your room. Putting a smooth texture directly next to a rough one while makes the rough object stand out more and seems weightier than if you space them apart. Use distance to determine how subtle a visual weight you would like to achieve.

Texture Provides Balance

Contrast is essential when it comes to design because it keeps things balanced and also provides visual interest. Think about it: If everything is too similar, our eyes will have trouble focusing and tend to glaze over. Use texture to make sure that your most important elements pop.

Restraint, of course, is also the key, so try not to go too texture-crazy. Stick to two or three distinct textures in any single space. Choose three when you want people to take in the space as a whole and stick to two when you want to emphasize a prominent focal point.

Texture is particularly important if you are working within a particular color palette where the shades are very similar. When a monochromatic or analogous color scheme, make sure you choose items that heavily contrast. When they come together, they will bring a sense of harmony to the space.

Using Texture At Home

All that reasoning as to why you should use texture is well and good, but it only goes so far if you don't know how to effectively bring it into your home. Here are a few ways that I would suggest to add texture to a room:

Architectural Elements: If you are lucky enough to have crown molding, chair rails, or tray ceilings in

your home, make them a focal point by using texture on those.

Furniture: Wooden benches, satin reading chairs, and marble tabletops all bring a distinct feel to the space.

Décor Items: Shadow boxes or flowers can be used.

Floor and Wall Coverings: A carefully placed throw rug or even some patterned wall design will bring tons of depth to the room.

Textiles: Use cloths like slipcovers, throw pillows, and even blankets to make the room pop.

But, if you would rather experiment digitally before buying, the Home Design 3D app lets you see how different colors and textures will look in your interiors – all via your smartphone.

Whether you choose a throw rug to warm up your bedroom or a wooden coffee table to bring life to your living space, the importance of texture is clear. It completes the room. Texture is the component that helps elevate your interiors to the next level. Don't be afraid of it in your own interiors. Instead, use it to create interiors that feel fit for a magazine.

Light: Light is an element that completes your interior design in all respect. Everything in place without a thought on light can spoil the whole interior. Light is used in Interior for three main purposes, Basic or general illumination, light for performing specific task-Task Light and the third one is Accent light, light to create mood and drama, emphasis, texture or depth in your design.

Nowadays, general lights like LEDs can also have different colors, intensity, provision to change as per your mood or desire. In the earlier days, light was used for study table, kitchen worktop, dressing table, bathroom mirror, etc, But nowadays, strips and linear sources are also used as task lights. To understand the necessity and effect of lighting in your design, you need to study what are the different kinds of lights. Those are a point source, Linear, Planer, Up lighter, Downlighter.

Now before we further proceed with the fundamentals of design, let us quickly remember the eight design elements studied in this chapter. Fill all the blanks with different elements you know.

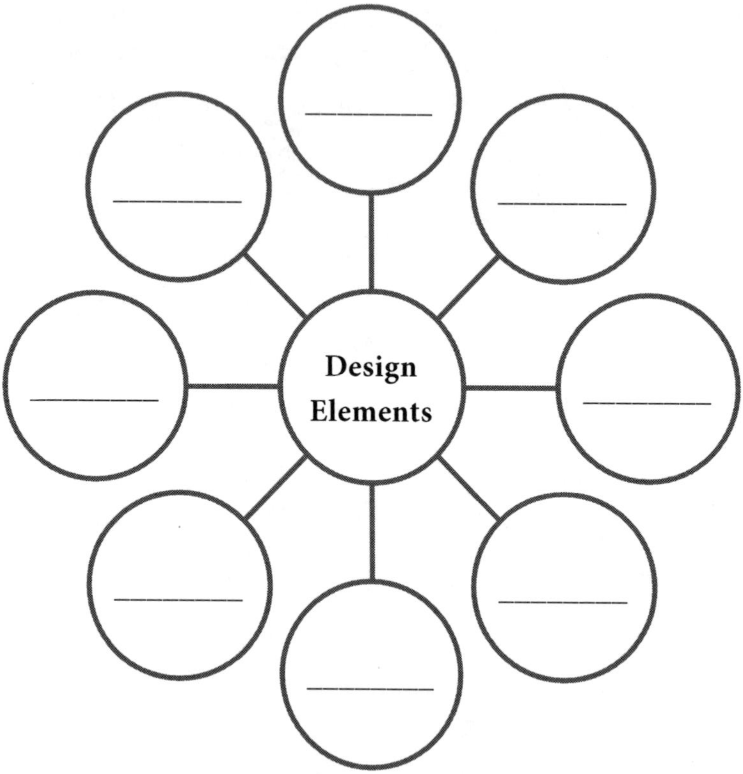

Know the Eighteen Design Principles!

Design fundamental also includes the principles of design. There are plenty of write-ups available on the internet to study this subject. Here, I am describing briefly for your understanding and what is sufficient to understand the design application. You will find 5 basic, 7 important, 9, 11 or 12 design principles on the internet. Actually, there are different thoughts on this. Here, I will discuss those principles only which are mostly used in Interior designing.

You need to use the elements of **art** and **design** – line, shape/form, space, volume, color, light and texture – to create a composition as a whole. The elements of art and design are the tools of visual artists and the principles will help you to organize all those elements in such a manner so that it becomes meaningful, functional and good to look or feel aesthetic.

1. ***Scale: Using the relative size*** of elements against each other can attract attention to a focal point.

When elements are designed larger than life, scale is being used to show drama. There are three different types of scales. Mechanical scale (described in technical drawing chapter), Human scale (Interior design and Architecture refers to this the most) and Visual scale (scale of space that can be changed by changing pattern, texture or color)

2. ***Balance*** is the key. It ensues the feeling of equivalence across a design space. Balance is the distribution of the visual weight of objects, colors, texture and space. If the design is a scale, these elements should be balanced to make a design feel stable. In symmetrical balance, the elements used on one side of the design are similar to those on the other side; in asymmetrical balance, the sides are different but still look balanced. In radial balance, the elements are arranged around a central point and may be similar.

3. ***Proportion*** conveys stability. It involves scaling of various elements to create a coherent design.

4. ***Unity:*** Unity refers to how well the elements of a design work together. Visual elements should have clear relationships with each other in a design. Unity also helps to ensure that concepts are being communicated in a clear and cohesive fashion. Designs with good unity also appear to be more organized and of higher quality and authority than the designs with poor unity.

5. ***Variety*** is what reaps the attention. It adds flavor to the design, making it more interesting and engaging. Without variety, a design can very quickly become monotonous, causing the user to lose interest. Variety can be created in a variety of ways, through color, typography, images, shapes, and virtually any other design element.

However, variety for the sake of variety is pointless. Variety should reinforce the other elements of a design and be used alongside them to create a more interesting and aesthetically pleasing outcome that improves the user's experience.

6. ***Rhythm:*** The spaces between repeating elements can cause a sense of rhythm to form,

It is similar to the way the space between notes in a musical composition creates a rhythm. There are five basic types of visual rhythms that designers can create: random, regular, alternating, flowing, and progressive.

Random rhythms have no discernable pattern. Regular rhythms follow the same spacing between each element with no variation.

Alternating rhythms follow a set pattern that repeats, but there is variation between the actual elements (such as a 1-2-3-1-2-3 pattern).

Flowing rhythms follow bends and curves, similar to the way sand dunes undulate or the waves flow.

Progressive rhythms change as they go along.

7. ***Harmony*** brings the elements closer. It utilizes familiar traits of design elements and puts them into focus.

8. ***Emphasis*** transports attention. It highlights the important parts and makes them standout. It is also known as Dominance. Dominance is created by contrasting size, positioning, color, style, or shape. The focal point should dominate the design with scale and contrast without sacrificing the unity of the whole.

9. ***Movement*** is what directs the eye. It leads the users to focus on an area in a design. The most important element should lead to the next most important and so on. This is done through positioning (the eye naturally falls on certain areas of a design first), emphasis, and other design elements already mentioned. Such movements can be directed along lines edges, shape and color within the design, and more.

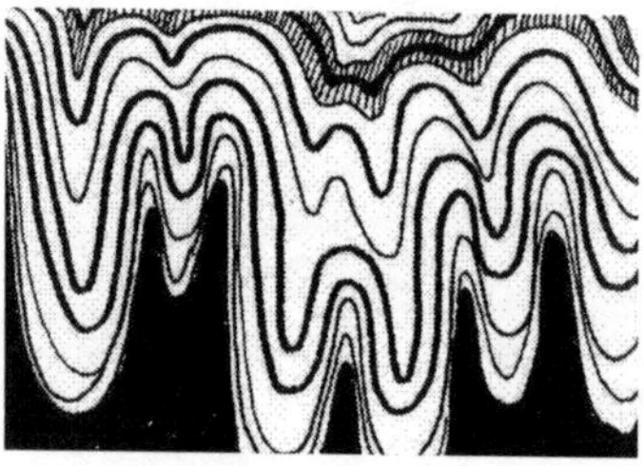

10. ***White Space,*** also referred to as "negative space" are the areas of a design that do not include any design elements. The space is, effectively empty.

Many new designers feel the need to pack every pixel with some type of "design" and overlook the value of white space. But white space serves many important purposes in a design, the foremost being giving elements of the design room to breathe. Negative space can also help in highlighting specific content or specific parts of a design.

11. ***Hierarchy*** means prioritizing the elements based on their importance. Hierarchy is typically created by creating a contrast between visual elements in a composition. Typically, visual elements with highest contrast are noticed first.

12. ***Repetition*** draws awareness to the design. It also brings consistency and flow to the design.

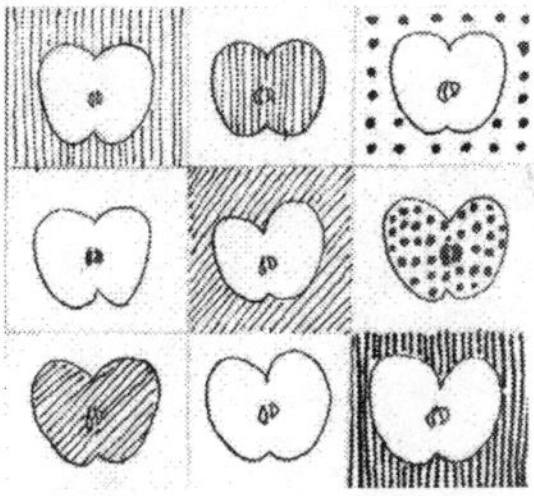

13. ***Pattern,*** builds the course. It builds familiarity and organizes design for trouble-free viewing.

14. ***Contrast*** addresses conflict. It highlights the difference and puts emphasis on what is important.

15. ***Progression*** can be defined as a type of rhythm as stated above and also its best described as the use of elements in a gradual rhythmic pattern by changing scale, resulting to change of the proportion repetitively.

16. ***Dominance:*** Things that are dominant have the most visual weight. They are the most important, powerful,

influential elements in your design. The principle of dominance is applied to how the different elements of design can be adjusted to give emphasis to an object.

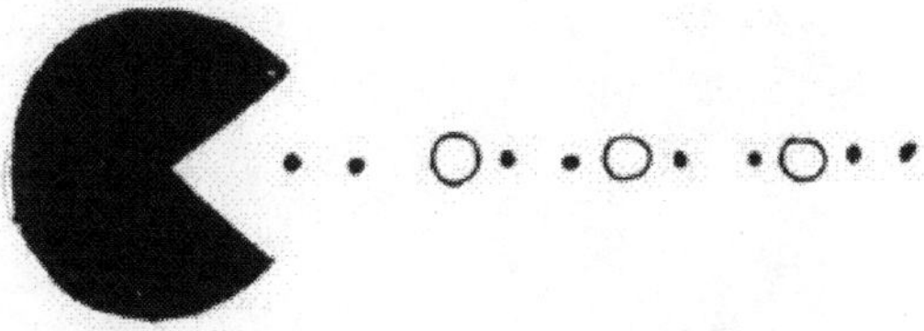

17. ***Proximity:*** When we are organizing information in our designs, we can use proximity to create relationships between elements to aid in understanding the information presented. For example, by grouping these images, we assign a relationship to the whole group.

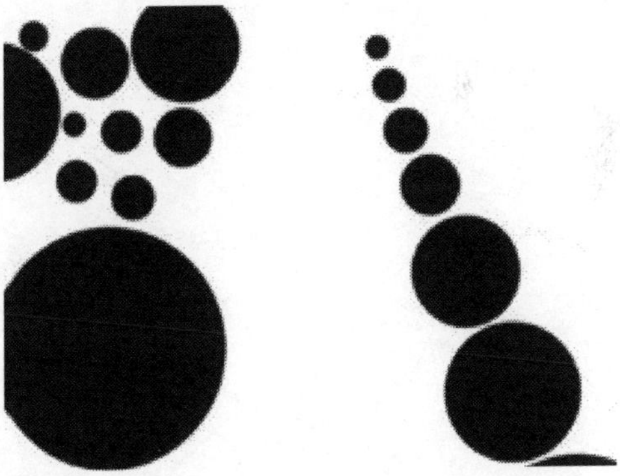

18. ***Alignment:*** The principle of alignment refers to the way the different elements in a design are lined up in relation to each other or to a particular part of

the space. When they are aligned with the side of the space, we call that edge alignment. Another alignment is center alignment.

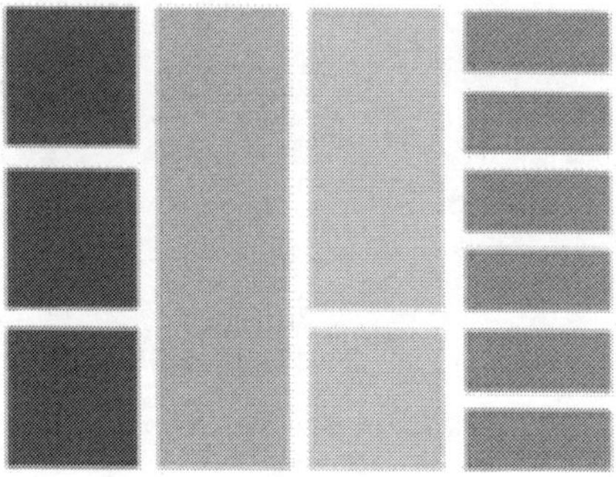

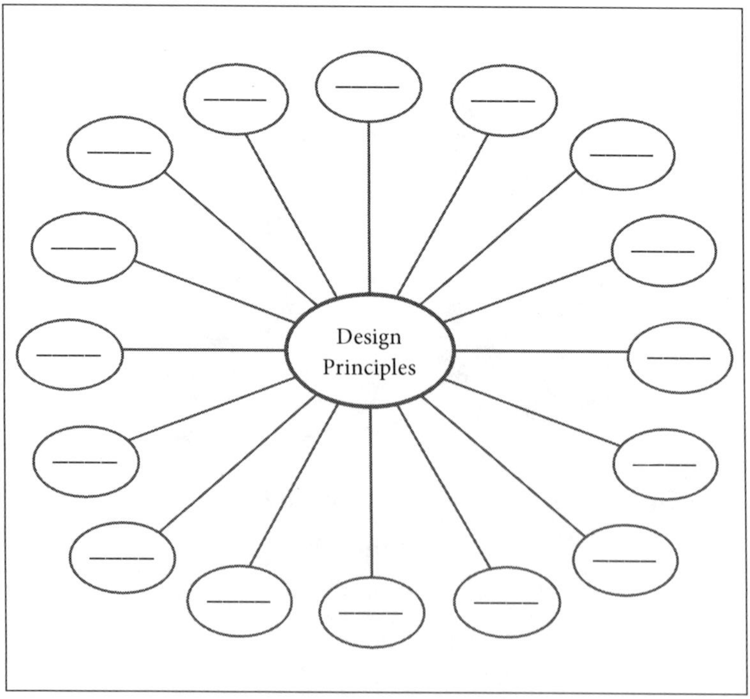

Now, by using the Eight Design Elements and Eighteen design principles you can practice some composition.

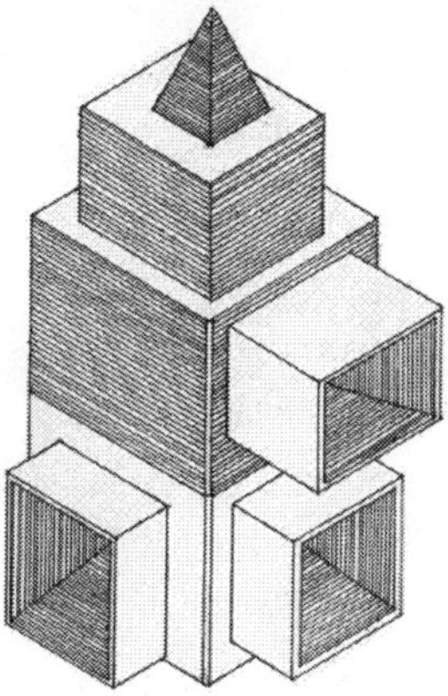

STEP 2

Be Inspired

In this chapter, I am going to answer a few important questions that are likely to surface in our mind when we try to find out Design inspiration.

Why is it important to be inspired? How to be inspired?

What is called design inspiration?

What are the sources of inspiration?

Can we create a concept from our inspiration? What is benchmark?

Why we need to differentiate our ideas and then copy directly

Signature style; what how and when?

To drive maximum output from this chapter, you need an inspiration board or mood board or concept board or design sketches.

While you want to become an Interior Designer, it is very much important to be inspired by some other work or history or Nature. Inspiration can also come from within in case you are an experienced designer. As a beginner, you have to search or seek inspiration for your new project. Try to understand there is nothing in this world that is not inspired by something or someone. Even if you are experienced enough in the field, during the design Decision Process for your new project, you must be inspired by some visuals you have already seen before on some similar projects you have done before. Or you must be inspired by some new ideas from something in the Nature you have never adopted in any of your earlier designs and want to try it for the first time. Whatever you may be, there will be a clear inspiration that can be triggered in each and every case. So, rather than being inspired unknowingly, it is very much important that you should be able to mark the inspiring facts or design consciously. Better to choose your inspiration with very much care and with appropriateness to your project.

In most cases, when you have a project or a problem in front of you either inspiration comes instantly or you have to wait a long day or week or even more than that to get the right inspiration. Mostly, if you have been waiting for the inspiration to reach you automatically someday or sometime, you are 100% not on the right track. 95% of the inspiration is activity driven. Once you get the project in your hand based on the character of the project and its type, you have to start searching different sources of inspiration. Design is common in nature across all the profession like Architecture, Fashion, Interior, Graphics, Jewelry, Sculpture, Painting etc.. Electrifying inspiration mostly comes when you are in a free mind. These could be the times when you are sleeping, in the bathroom, driving or having a cup of tea while sitting in your balcony. What it actually means is that when your brain is not so busy with the day-to-day practical problems, these are the perfect time to get inspired for your current project. And this 5% plays a major role in your design.

So, when some ideas, innovations or inspiration comes do not forget to take a pen and paper and document it. It is important to write in black and white because this type of thought never comes back or we canot really remember later. Even if you have a good memory, it might be lost during the course of day-to-day activities. So do not wait to document your inspiration, documenting it right away can help you get a more detailed understanding so you can start brainstorming on that inspiration instantly.

A design inspiration needs not to be another design. It can be anything like any object, history, any moment, any visuals, any thought, any document or anything that your brain is able to convert into design ideas.

Now talking about the different sources of design inspiration, 95% of ideas that hatch are either from your experience knowledge, intelligence and hard work or a combination of all these. Now you can try out different sources of books and magazines in the relevant field which is a good source.

The work of other good designers can also inspire you. Design is common in nature across all the professions, fashion galleries, graphics, culture sculpture, interiors, architectural, paintings, etc. So you may find your design project inspiration from a dress designed by some fashion designer or painting done by a painter. You already know the Fundamentals of design light elements and principles, so you can adopt any inspiration from any source into your project. Another source of inspiration is past history. These could be errors and their design characters or the practices used to design a modern interior. Sometimes your clients can also guide you from where to take the inspiration.

The best practice in design is to be inspired by Nature as in our Nature, there is no similar shape, color or texture for lighting effects. If you can get your inspiration from Nature about the leaves or a particular tree, you will notice that they do not always have the same shape. So, if the shapes can vary from one leaf to another, the color can also be different, the detailing, the orientation; everything is different. Hence, it is very much easier to be inspired by nature.

Inspiration Board

Mood Board

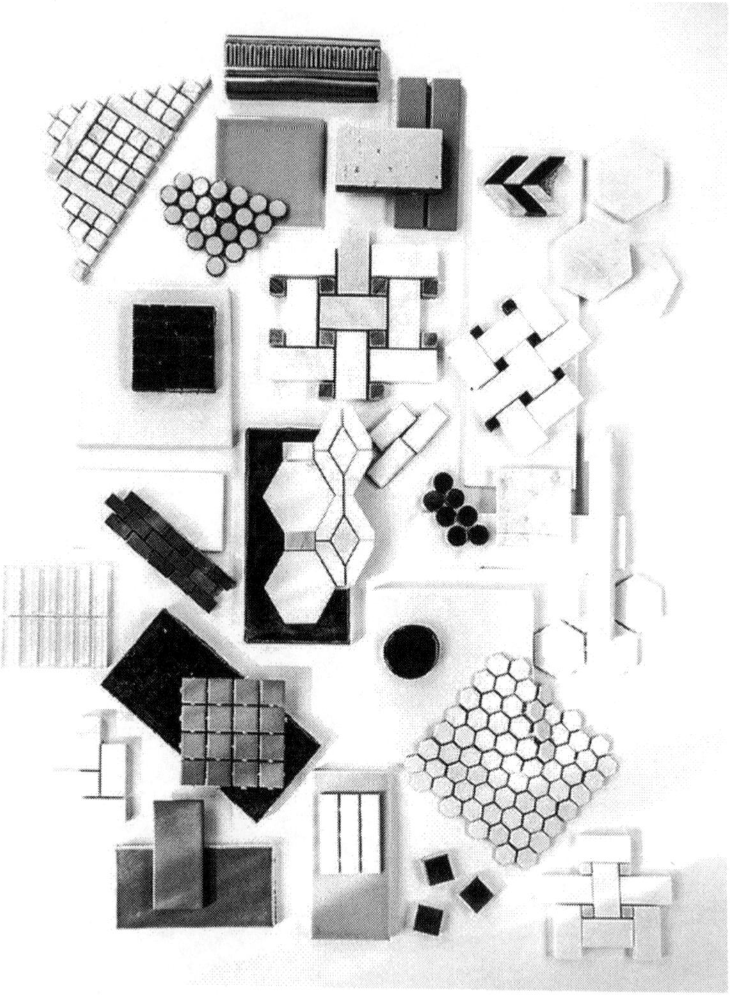

Material Board

STEP 3

Be Technical

Dear readers, please do not feel horror-struck after reading the title of this chapter as technical. At the beginning of this book, I have promised to help you learn technical drawing without being very much technical.

But yes, it is very much important to be able to express your thought to your client as well as your vendor, contractor, and suppliers. Here in this chapter, I will help you learn the step-by-step method for being able to draw and understand technical drawings easily. Once you can read a technical drawing, you will be able to communicate the same to others. So in this chapter, you will learn the following:

Why is it necessary to be able to read technical drawings? What do the so-called technical drawings mean?

What are the different forms and methods of drawing technically? How to present your thought through technical drawings?

How to make your drawing more presentable, readable, attractive and at the same time perfectly technical sufficient for practical execution?

Let's start with why is it necessary to know technical drawing.

In Interior design practice, it is mandatory for everyone practicing interior design to be able to produce a set of drawings for flawless execution. Though changes in scope hamper the project execution and at that time, you may have to take an on-spot decision to sidestep delay or connect the drawings to make it practical based on the site condition, detailing or client's request. Still, in the beginning, you need to prepare the set of drawings to get approval from the client, to do the Estimation and Costing, to understand the look and feel of that space, to get and compare quotations from different vendors, to calculate the quantity of each material and also to reduce the supervision time and number of site visits. Technical drawing also helps us prevent much changes in the design once the design is frozen by the client. So you have to learn technical drawing sufficiently to express your thoughts and ideas to all the stakeholders.

Now there are different methods to draw a proper

technical drawing. As per the engineering practices third-angle-projection, plan, elevation, section, isometric views, axonometric views, etc. are known as technical drawing which is covered in the descriptive geometry segment. But don't worry, as I have promised at the beginning that any layman with a bit understanding in drawing or passion in design can learn this. Here, we will practice on a simple graph paper or a grid. So, let's start.

First, take a cube or a dice. To understand the plan and elevation, you need to know about different types of 3-dimensional simple geometric objects. These have already been explained in the first chapter; "be passionate", under design elements. If you have missed you can go back and check.

Dice is the basic three-dimensional object and very easy to understand from different angles. If you keep the dice on a table and try to see it exactly from the top, you will be able to see a square. This view from the top is called the plan view. Now you try to see the same dice from all four sides one by one and you will be able to see the same Square from all sides. The object from right is called right side elevation, from left it is called left side elevation. As the dice or cube looks the same from all sides, so let's practice the same with another object which is not similar from all sides. Take your mobile and put it on the table, now try to see it from the top and from all four sides. You will find different 2D geometrical shapes. From the top it is a rectangle, from the side it is a small thin rectangle, from the front and back you will see long thin rectangles. Look at the figure below.

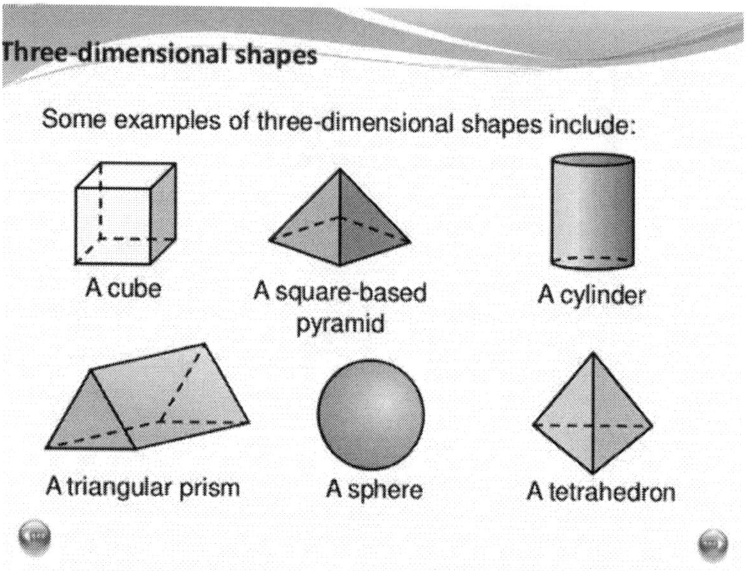

Now let's practice with a cylindrical object like the mineral water bottle or a can or a glass. Trust me, this is a foolproof plan to teach even school children about plan and elevation. And I have practiced this with lots of school students from class 8 to 12 and more. Now let's keep a bottle or a can on the top of the table. What can you see from the top? Yes, it is a circle, in case of the can and in case of bottle you can see two circles with the same Centre but a different radius. The bottom circle can also be seen with the top circle presenting the bottle and cap. So this is the plan. See the figure below.

From any side of the can, you can see a rectangle only in 2D. The bottle is having a unit shape which canot be defined by any existing name. So now you are becoming more knowledgeable about understanding elevations. Practically plan is having two dimensions on axis X and Y whereas elevation is having two dimensions again on either axis X and Z or Y and Z.

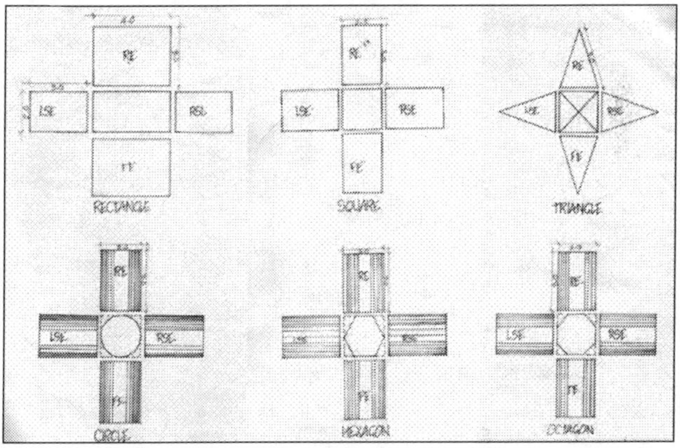

Fig. 1

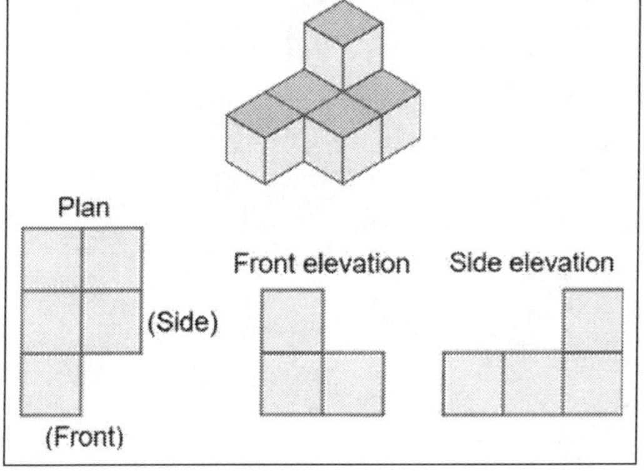

Fig. 2

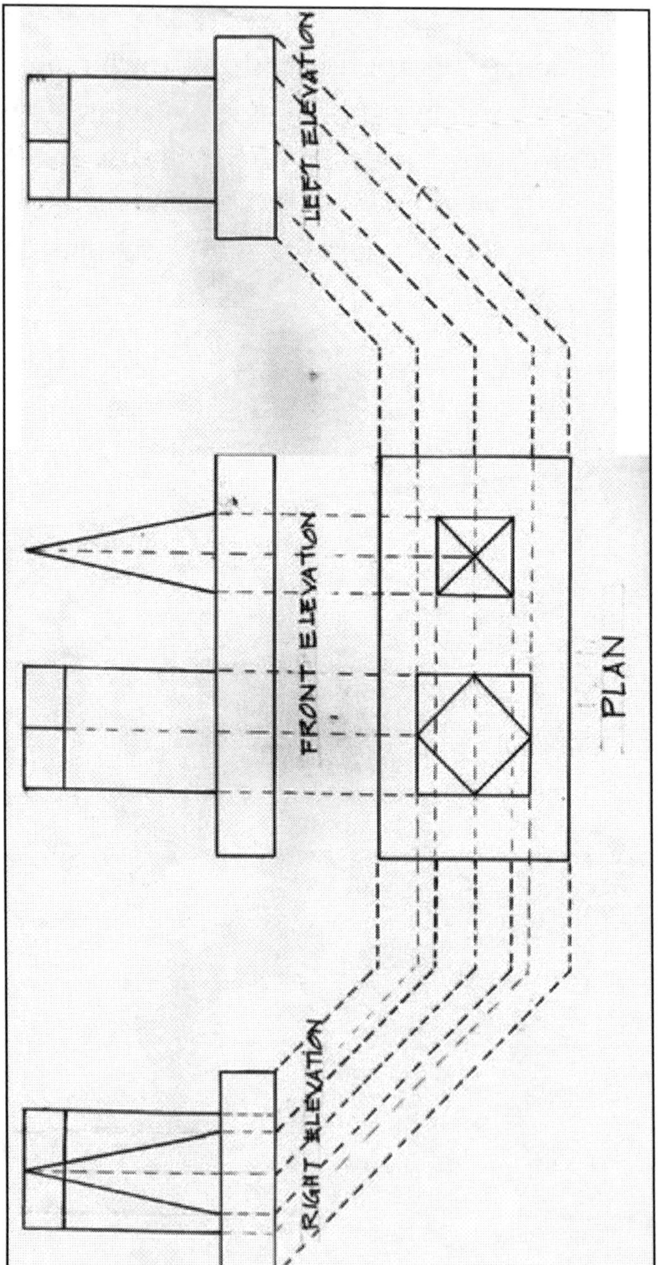

Fig. 3

Now, let's switch to a complex object. Put two or three simple objects together and try to draw plan and elevations for the same. Instead of using third angle projection as you might not know, you can use a simple graph paper. One has been done below for your understanding.

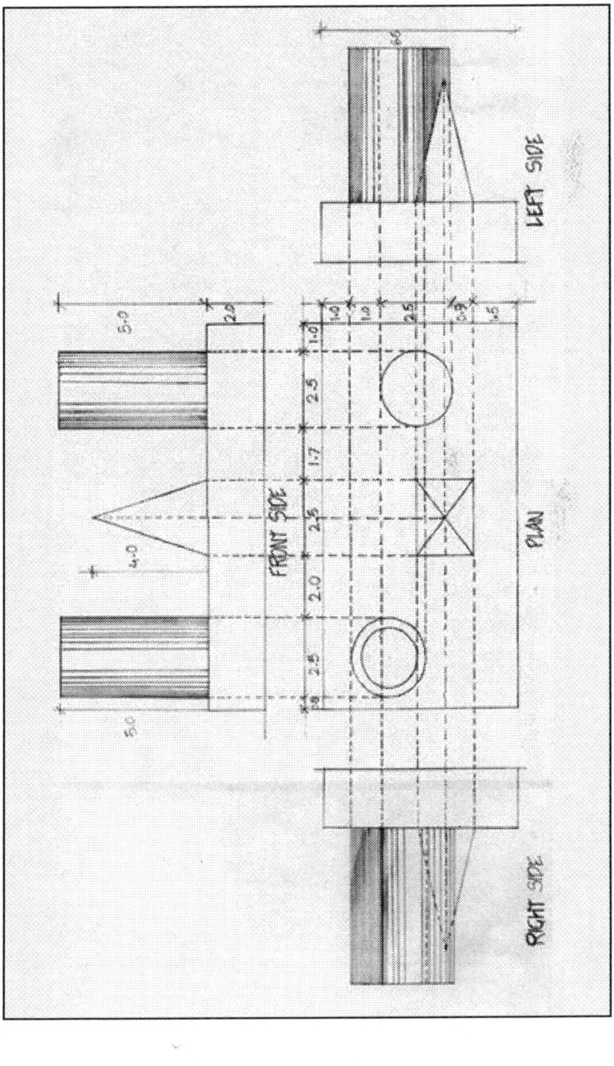

Fig. 4

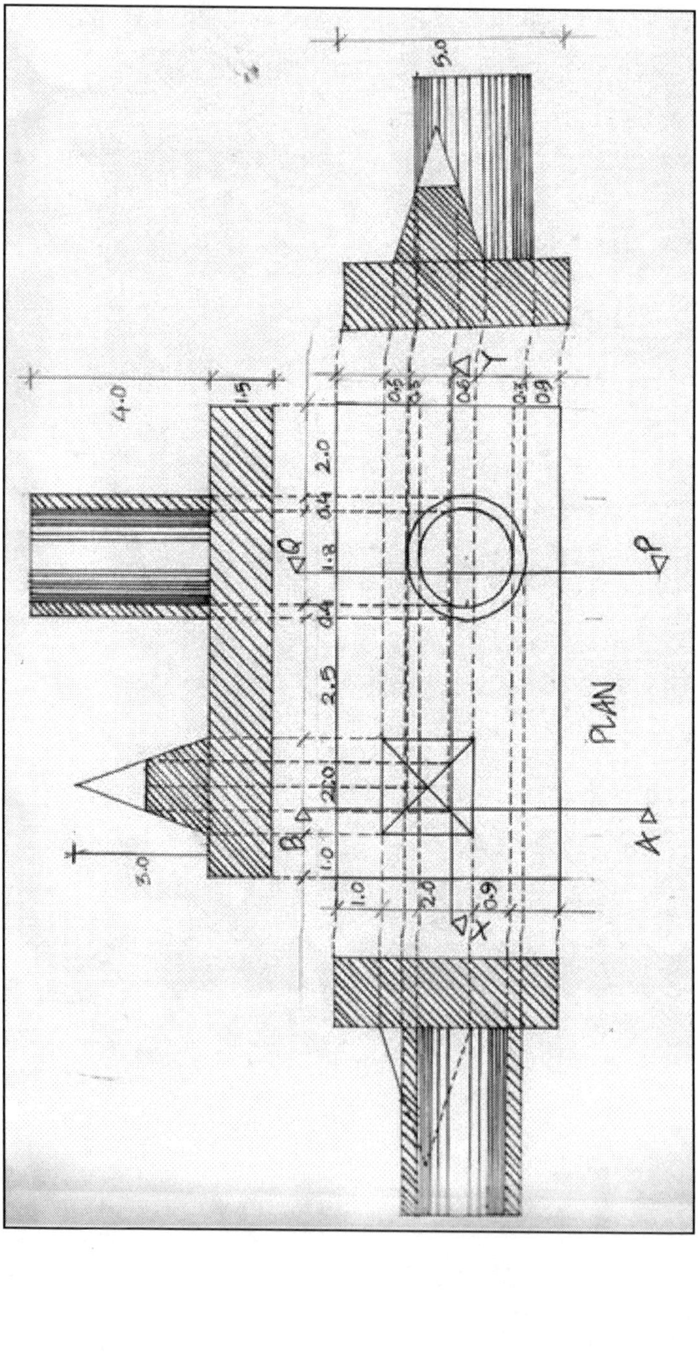

Fig. 5

Now start looking for a room or a space. Here, I am giving you a set of a plan and elevation. If you are able to identify the objects and find out all the mistakes then you have become an expert in reading a technical drawing. Once you can read a drawing, you can also produce your own drawing by using the same graph paper or grid. Let's take the test. The figure below is having 3 mismatches, find out and match with elevations.

Fig. 6

Once you have understood the plan and elevation completely, you can now draw a plan and elevation for your project. Once you have completed drawing your plan and elevation, it is mandatory to present the same with colored renderings to make it more interesting and understandable. For this, you just need to practice on an existing layout for plan and elevation like the figure below. Use good quality wood pencil colors. Here, we will discuss a few techniques of graphic representation. There are a few rules or practices that you need to follow while you are rendering your 2D drawing. Find out the steps below.

The thickness and type of lines represent a different meaning in technical drawing.

- Thick and bold continuous line represents the object.
- Objects closer to your eyes are thicker than the object far away from your eyes.

- The hidden Part of the objects that are not visible practically is represented with a dashed line or hidden line.
- To represent the central axis central line or dash and dot line are used.

Few objects which you need to fill up with hatches should be very thin in thickness. A different kind of Hatch used to represent different kinds of materials. A ready reckoner chart for your reference is added here.

Sr. No.	Type of line	Thickness (mm)	Illustration	General Application
1	Continuous thick	0.5	Thick	Visible outlines
2	Continuous thin	0.2	Thin	Dimension lines, extension lines, projection lines, leader lines, hatching, revolved section, construction lines etc
3	Dashed medium thick	0.3	Medium Thick	Hidden Line
4	Chain thin	0.2	Thin	Centre line, lines of symmetry
5	Chain thin and thick at end only	0.2 for thin & 0.5 for thick ends	Thin	Cutting plane lines
6	Continuous thin wavy	0.2	Thin	Irregular boundary lines
7	Continuous thin with zig-zags	0.2	Thin	Long break line
8	Continuous thin and arrow- heads at both ends	0.2	Thin	Dimension lines

Pic. 1

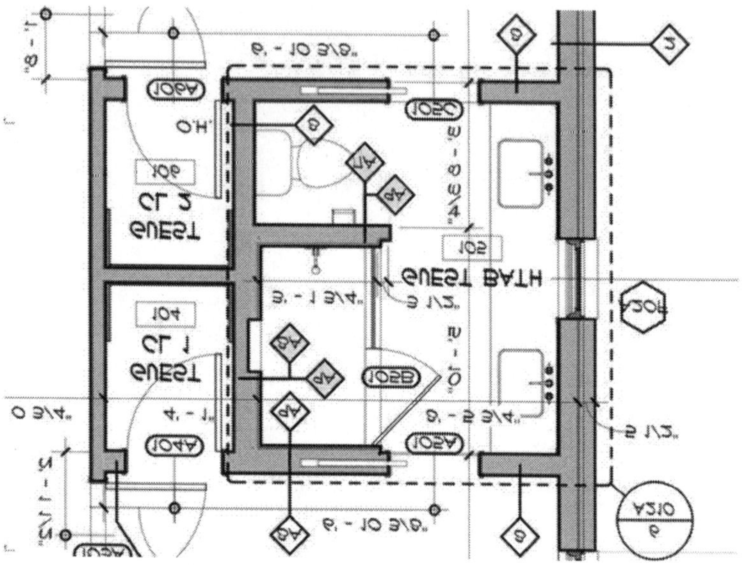

Pic. 2

Like different types of lines, thicknesses, hatches, there are some specific colors used in practice. Try to color your drawing as you are applying on the flooring walls, furnishings, bedspread coverings, etc.

Once you are done with Plan and Elevation, now its time to understand the Sections. To create a room plan and elevation, actually, you have learned to create a section too. Let me explain. Think of a room with a roof slab on the top. If we see from the top we should be able to see only a square or rectangle. No details like furniture can be seen. So, to see those, we have taken a slicer and sliced through all the four walls at a particular height or elevation from the floor. Normally we take it at 1 mt.

above the floor level. Therefore, some of the elements like wall, door and windows got cut and some other low height furniture like bed, table, etc. are lying below that line and are visible. Some features like light, fan, ceiling decorations, etc. are above the line and we can't see in the same drawing. So here the elements cut through are in the section, the elements lying on floor uncut are in elevation and for the elements, we can't see, we can create another layout that will be a reflected plan. For the ceiling, we call it RCP or reflected ceiling plan. Graphically, the walls, door and windows that got cut, we show with hatches filled in represent objects in section and rest are objects in elevation.

In case of wall elevations, the same logic applies. The wall we are showing is cut through an invisible slicer at a specific distance from that particular wall and that should be marked on the plan through which we are cutting the plain. So the interior elevations are called Sectional elevation. Now you can understand the meaning of hatches in the previous drawing. By this time, you should be able to differentiate between the types of objects in the section and elevation and relate. You can practice with some complex geometrical 3-dimensional shapes given here.

The last part of technical drawing is 3-dimensional views like Isometric and Axonometric views. It has been described in detail in the next 3D chapter.

STEP 4
Think In 3D

In this chapter, I am going to tell you the following:

Why 3-dimensional drawing is important?

What are the different types of 3-dimensional drawings? How to draw one-point perspective?

How to draw two-point perspective?

How to draw Isometric or Axonometric drawing?

Imagination is never 2D i.e. two dimensional. It is always 3D, which means 3-dimensional. The human brain can see only 3-dimensional forms of sceneries or objects. Basically, 2-dimensional drawings are non-existent and created by humans after following certain geometrical rules. Whereas, 3 dimensional drawings are easy to visualize, understand and express. Also, it is possible to get an idea from a 3-dimensional drawing for a non-technical person too. So it is always preferable to represent your ideas in 3D and develop a workable and detailed drawing in 2D.

Therefore, why not present your ideas also in 3D? Do not be afraid of 3D sketches. Till you reach the end of this chapter, you will know all the tips and tricks of expressing your ideas. In the case of room interior, first, understand what a room or space means. It‘s an enclosure of what? The three major elements to enclose are wall, floor and ceiling. You can show your design, concept or detail in three ways; either by one-point perspective, two-point perspectives or by isometric design. There are various other ways like three-point perspective, axonometric, etc. Here you need not go in that much detail only a few one-point, two-point and isometric drawing with proper graphical representation can be enough for you to express your ideas to your client.

First, you decide which element or elements you want to show/present. You should show that particular wall on the floor and on the ceiling which is having more elements or things to show. Accordingly, if you have one major wall with floor and ceiling, you must go for one-point perspective for three walls since one-point perspective is more appropriate. The perspective view is good to express but not to execute. This is because it does not have a proper scale or dimensions, it depends on the eye or camera positioning, vertical and horizontal plane, etc. So another way of expressing yourself in 3D is the isometric view. These views have a proper measurement, are easy to understand and draw.

Here I will share with you some thumb rules to draw all these three for which you need not be an engineer or a very good artist. I would like to tell you another thing that in our society we think good artists can become very good designers or Architects. This is partially right. Lots of people in our society have good observation, imagination, power, knowledge and are also passionate about the subject but they do not know how to express. Artists develop all these qualities with talent and practice of expressing themselves. So you need not worry, even if one is not very good at drawing, one can draw by using proper methods.

One-Point Perspective:-

The concept of one-point perspective can be understood best by the example of the railway track or long distant highway or roads.

Photo of railway track

Photo of road

From a distance, all horizontal parallel planes seem to be not parallel but trying to meet at a point or as if generated from one single point. The same is applicable for the interior view too.

1. Take a readymade graph paper from the market or you can draw a few equal grids on a white paper. Note: draw the grid centrally so that you can extend walls all around.

2. Assume one grid as 1’ or draw one rectangle as shown. That is the wall in front of us.

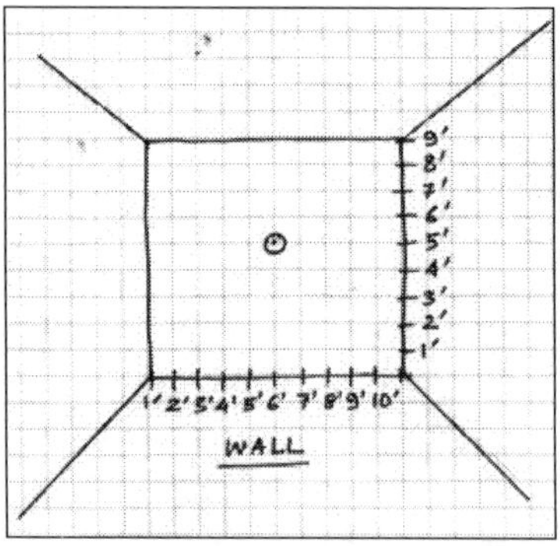

Fig. 1 (Wall)

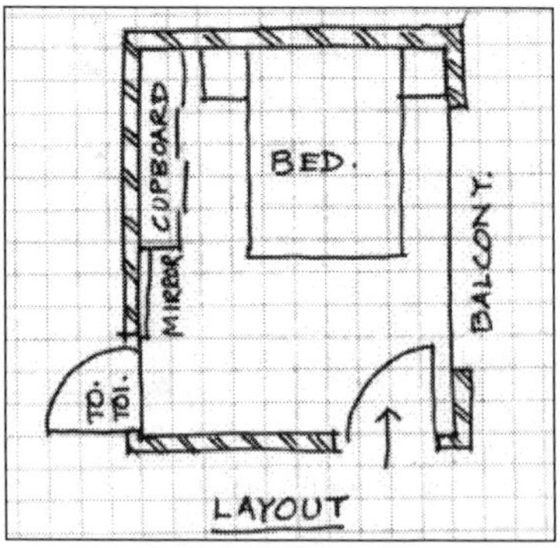

Fig. 2 (Layout)

If your room size is 10‘x12‘ and major wall i.e. the main furniture is placed along 10‘ and the room height is 9‘, you have to draw a 10‘x9‘ grid in the center.

3. Human eyes are placed at a height of 5‘ as per Indian standard. Indian human figure is 5‘6” on an average.

So our eye plane is at 5'. Mark a point @ 5' on the vertical grid.

Here you have to finalize the horizontal placement of the eye. Let's say, if you want to show the main wall + right wall more and left wall less then you have to stand towards left walls, the horizontal eye position will also be towards left. If you want to show the left wall more with the central wall then the eye positioning will be towards the right. Check in the Fig. below.

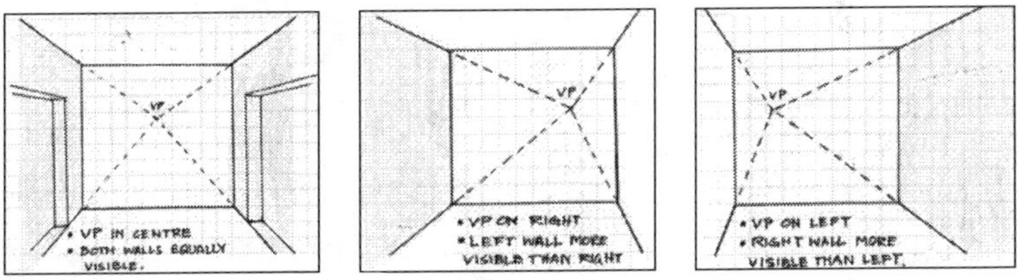

Fig. 3

4. After proper positioning of the eye i.e. the point of 1st point perspective view, join 4 corners of the main wall and extend outside till it looks good, means till it does not appear distorted. 3 walls, part ceiling and part floor are constructed.

5. Now you need to decide the visibility limit of the floor. Here methods are there but we shall try in a simple way. Just use a bit of your imagination, proportion

and sense of scale to decide the floor. Try to watch the floor dimensions ft. with the help of a compass.

So if width = 10‘ then approximate ft. is also equal to 10‘ can be imagined. Now join C with B.

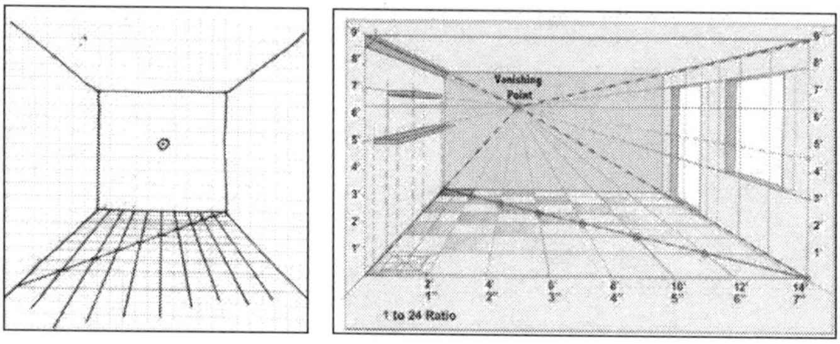

Fig. 4

Join all the four points of vertical grids on AB with eyepoint P and extend on the floor. Your view will look like fig. 4.

6. Now draw horizontal lines through each cut point of lines generated from P on the floor plane and diagonal lines B C. You will get 1‘x1‘ grid on the floor too. Only the grid will appear smaller in distance and bigger when close. In reality, it looks like the same.

   For walls, you can create grids in a similar way.

7. Architects and designers normally start putting furniture and elements after this.

However, for a non-technical person, I would suggest to draw all the grids on a paper first then start with the furniture layout.

So now, try to draw the sidewall grids. Here on the sidewall, a vertical grid will be generated from the floor grid endpoints. As shown in fig. 5. For horizontal grids, you need to join point P with the endpoint of horizontal grids on the main/central wall AB.

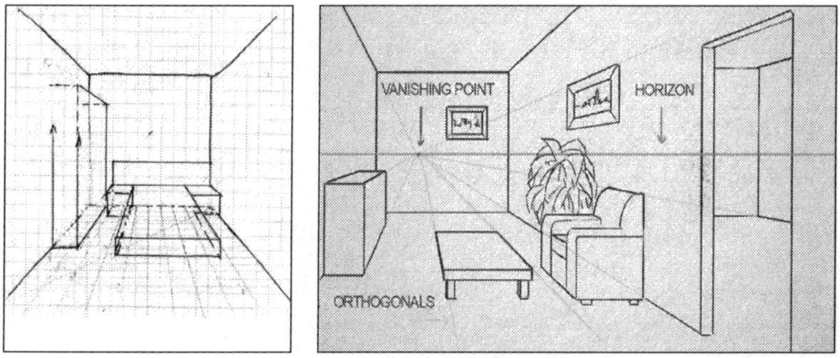

Fig. 5

Now you can try this with cuboids. You can use a box of paste or a television set-top box. To understand the cylindrical object, you can try a glass, talcum powder, Pepsi can, etc. For a conical object, you can observe placing a birthday cap on a table. After a thorough study of a simpler object, you can try some complex objects as shown. Place a glass on a box, place another cube also. Now try looking from different sides. See the examples below. Change the position of smaller objects and try to sketch all views again. As much as you will practice this, your understanding of a plan and elevation will increase.

Two-point Perspective:-

Kitchen

Living Room

Bed Room

Now let us learn how to draw a two-point perspective. In the earlier section, you have learnt to draw one-point perspective view. Sometimes you will find some important elements that are there in your design, to show them, you need to show only two walls apart of ceiling and floor, or you can say a corner of a room or space having important elements can be represented by a two-point perspective.

Like one–point, here also you have a viewing plane @ a height of approx. 5‘6” on which there will be two vanishing points on each side. With the variable height of your viewing plane or eye height, you can have various types of 2-point perspective. I have tried to make the process easy and with bare minimum efforts that are sufficient to express your design. So, by using the graph again let us learn how we can express our design in an understandable and presentable fashion.

1. Take a corner point A’ on a graph.
2. From A’ we need to generate a corner of the wall, two sides of walls and floor. To do that take a vertical line

up to 9/10 grids that match with the ceiling height of your room.

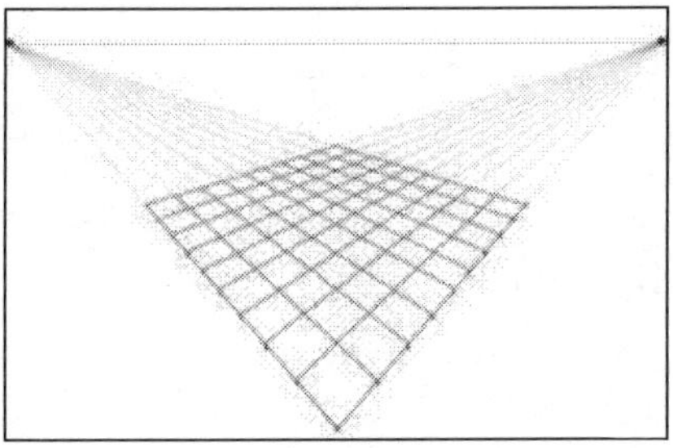

3. Now draw a horizontal line through 5 or 5 ½ grid above point A. Make it as long as possible so that your two vanishing points are far from each other.

By positioning the vanishing point far means you will be able to draw a less distressing view. You can practice on a few graphs by placing the vanishing points at various distances from each other.

4. Take a scale to join point A and one vanishing point and extend beyond A side.

5. Do the same for point A and add another vanishing point. Now, these two lines are the bottomof two walls you are going to detail out.

6. Draw a line between point B and vanishing point 1 and vanishing point 2 in a similar way and extend. Now you can clearly see both the walls with a profile of the ceiling too.

7. Now the main part of Two-point perspective is to be able to visualize the floor layout and the scale of the same. Take two points C and E on two-floor lines on the same horizontal grid and join. This is the line till which you will be able to see all elements on the floor without any major distortion, you will see a distorted view of objects beyond this line. So be careful while taking the horizontal line.

8. Now you need to join both C and E with alternative vanishing points so that a 3- dimensional floor appears on the drawing. You can show A-C-D-E on the floor of the room or space.

9. Divide CE into equal size and a multiple numbers of segments using the background graph. Join all those dots from both vanishing points 1 and 2. It will form a grid on the floor.

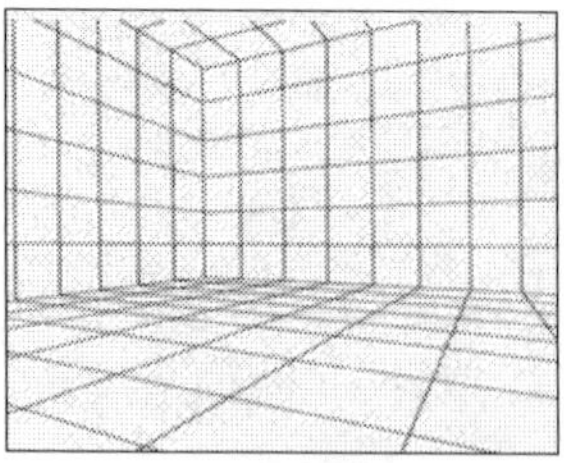

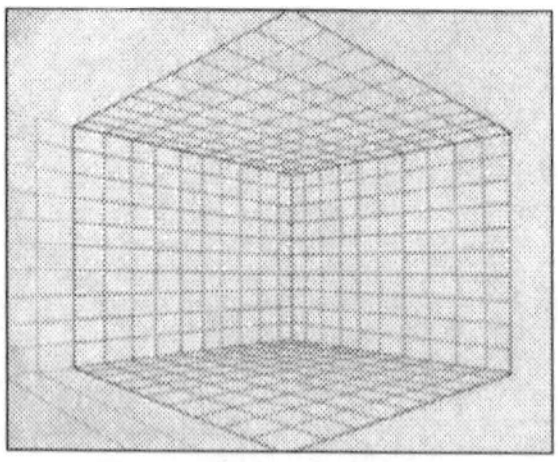

10. Now you can plot your room layout on this floor grid and then add heights to your furniture or elements.

11. To add heights to your layout, you need to have a vertical scale as well. That can be marked with dots AB, each grid represents one foot.

12. So to get a height of a bed, let's say 1'6", you need to join X with both vanishing points and extend on walls so that you will receive the height of bed at different points of the layout.

13. You just need to draw a vertical line at all four corners of the bed and match with the lines coming from vanishing point to that location.

14. Similarly, you can generate different heights for different elements, extend, take vertical from the actual location on layout and join. Repeat this for each object.

15. Once you finish drafting all objects, you need to see that objects placed near you may cover objects placed far away if having more heights. Accordingly, you have to either erase the unseen lines or you have to face the lines that are visible.

16. To add life to your perspective views never forget to add some features like a painting on wall, a curtain for door or window, ceiling heights or fan, ACs, a table lampshade on floor on table, a planter with a plant, furnishings, decoration like wallpaper or painting, an artifact and last but not least a human figure. All these elements add life to your presentation. Ceiling and floor grid you can also keep it applicable

Now your two-point perspective view is ready. Whether you know CAD or not, any other technical drawings or not, you can now easily present your thoughts in 3D to your client.

Please find the Do's and Don't's for 2-Point perspective views

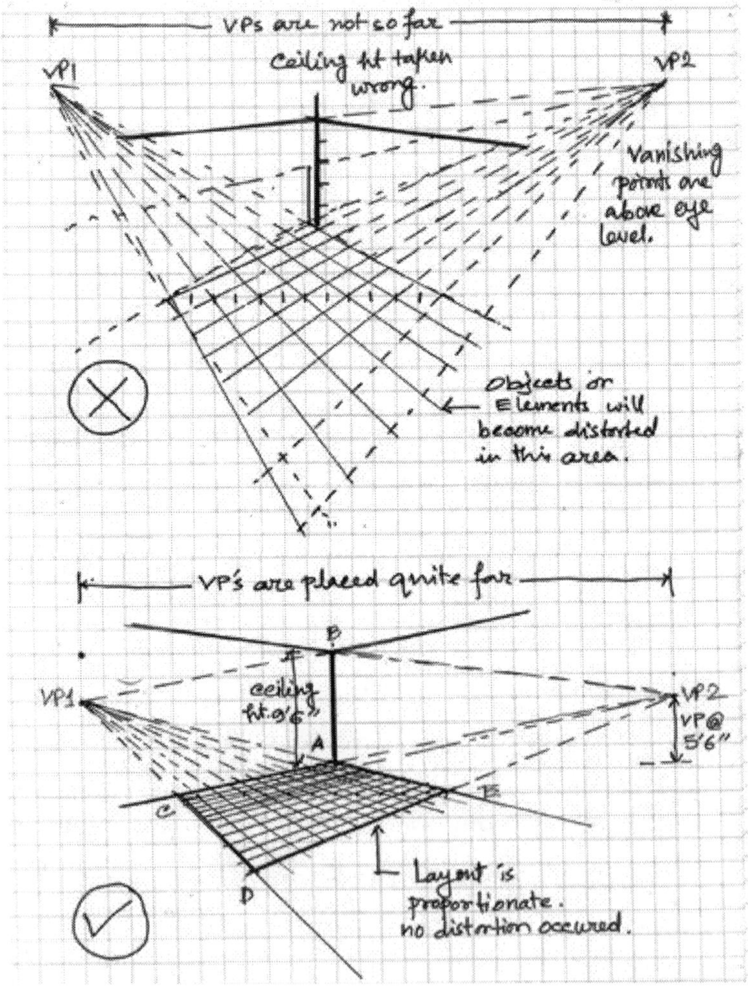

For more details, you can visit www.olgaart888.com. Here is one for you. Now try this.

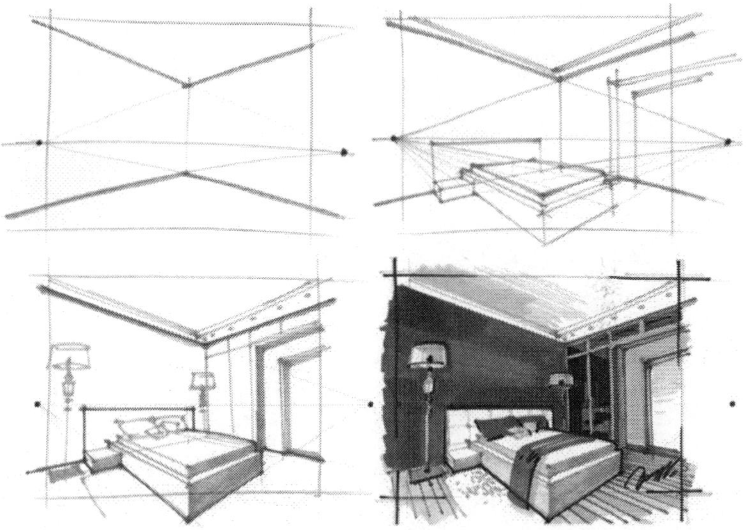

Isometric and Axonometric view:-

First, please make it clear that these methods are an imaginary representation of the objects. We can never see an object like these. Our brain can only view objects and sceneries in perspective and with multiple vanishing points which are very difficult to draw with the help of engineering drawing.

So, Isometric or axonometric drawings are just a representation of the object for manufacturing, execution and visualization purposes.

Axonometric views are drawn in three different ways. Let's take a cube and try to understand from the picture below. If all the three edges are drawn equally with two equal angles, these are called Isometric. Whereas, if two horizontal edges are equal but the vertical is not then it is called diametric and if all three edges are drawn in different sizes, it is called trimetric.

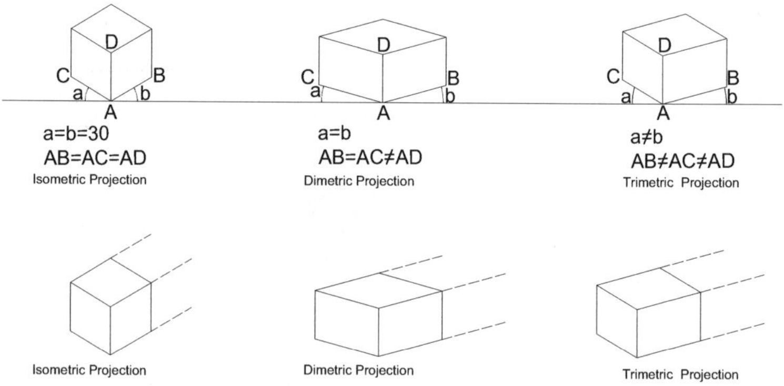

To understand these, you can again take a dice or cube and place it on the table. Place the cube diagonally, keeping both the angles equal to the central axis. The height of the object is perpendicular to the table. This is called Isometric view (both angles are equal). If you place one edge of dice parallel to your eyes and on the table, with second edge angular, it is called Axonometric view. In both cases, the height or elevation or z-axis is perpendicular to the table.

Please note, in reality, these views never can be seen in the same way. Our eyes always see an object having edges vanishing towards an unknown long-distant point. And those views are called Perspective views, which are covered in the next chapter. The purpose of Isometric or Axonometric view is to guide the labour with the 3rd dimension of any object or furniture that is not visible either in plan or elevation. So it is also necessary to practice these views as well. Here are some Isometric and Axonometric views of furniture for you.

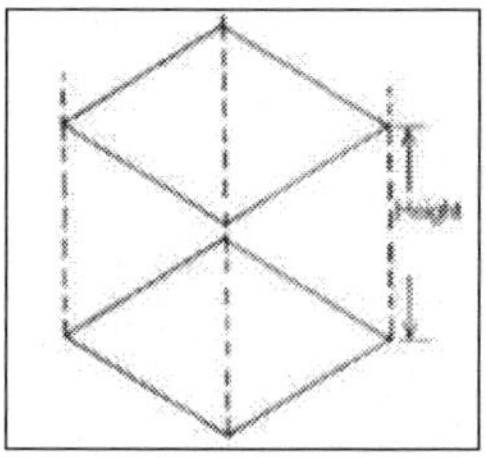

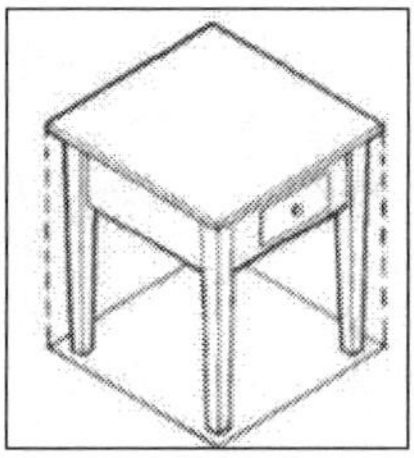

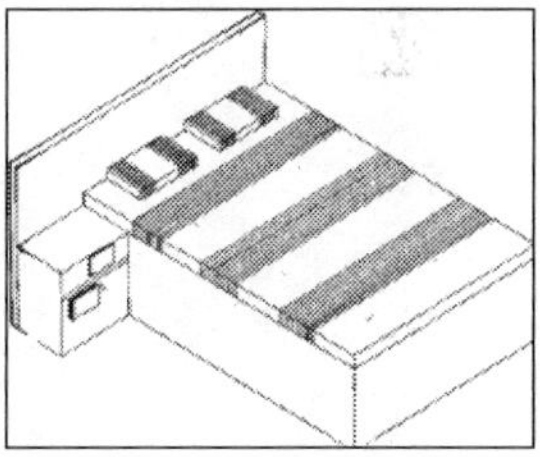

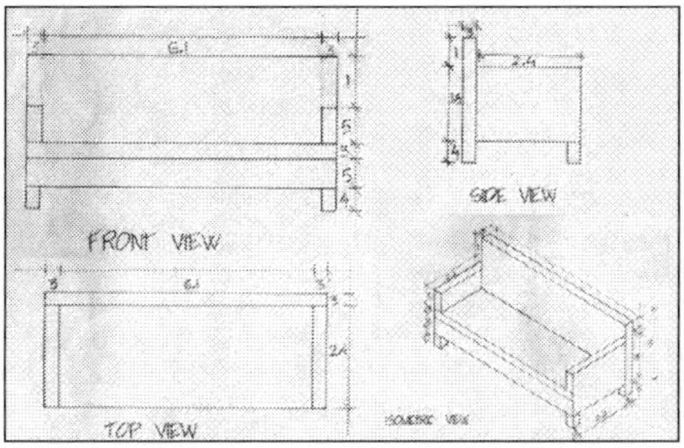

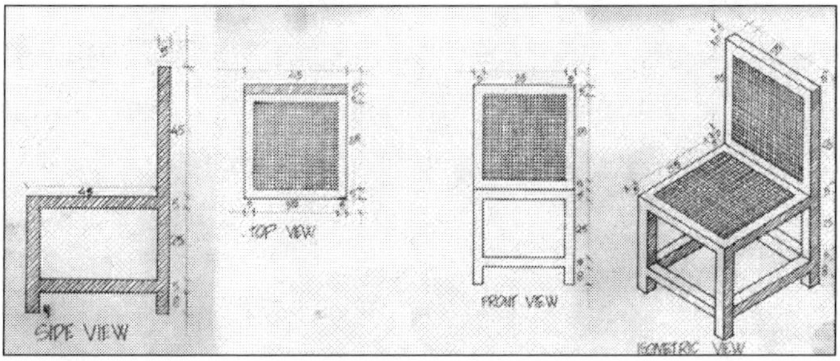

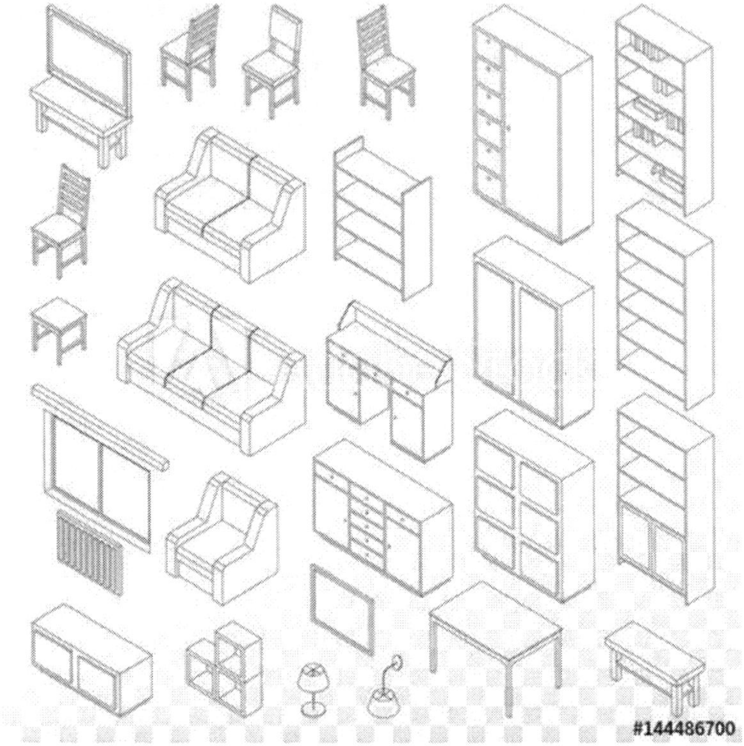

For more examples, please refer to Adobe stock, Pinterest, Shutter stock, etc.

So now you can express your design with any of the methods described here; 2-dimensional or 3- dimensional. You know 2D drafting. So to draft a room you need to know plan and elevation and sections of the buildings. You should know about the sizes of different building materials. The detailed knowledge of materials is shared in chapter 7.

STEP 5

Be Decisive

Space Planning (Be Innovative And Calculative)

While you are trying to do effective space planning, you might face various challenges. Most designers, nowadays, face the problem of space constraints. Today's requirement is to design everything in a smaller space. Basic human needs fit in a space smaller than it is required. Let us take an example. If you compare the Historical buildings that evolved through colonial buildings, modern houses/ apartments and Studio apartments you can easily understand how this space crunch has been happening in today's world.

Historical buildings used to have a single room or you can say a hall of minimum 60 Feet by 30 feet whereas in the colonial buildings you find a room of size having 30 by 20 feet, in case of modern houses sizes evolved from 15 by 20 to 12 by 10 and finally, now you have to accommodate the entire functions like sleeping, storage and living together in a single space named as Studio apartments having a size of maximum 20 feet by 12 feet.

Now that's the challenge since you have to accommodate based on the client's priority. Well, the tricks lie in your innovation here.

Starting from being passionate about design and being inspired, this is the stage where you have to be innovative.

In this chapter, I am going to discuss the actual methodology to mine a good solution for your project problem sum. Let me take you to the next step of design through an example. In the above matrix the family A,

Family – A:-

- Husband, wife and one kid (son) age group of 12 years.
- Housewife cooks herself
- Housewife takes care of son's education. She teaches her son.

The landlady is a housewife who cooks herself and also takes care of her son herself. So you can easily guess her role that if she needs to manage both she will not prefer to travel much between kitchen and son's bedroom. It gives you a clear idea about the necessity of keeping these two areas close to each other. Now your common sense says that the kitchen should be adjacent to the dining area, activity-wise, and privacy-wise no bedroom can be placed in a public or semi-private zone. So here you have to have a semi adjacent arrangement and a short distance travel space between the kitchen and son‘s bedroom. So it is very much clear that here you can create a small lobby or a passage between these two to minimize the travel time, maximize the control and keeping the privacy level appropriate.

You may think that once you have created one matrix, activity chart or similar with some number

and age group family, you can use the same for another. However, you have to be more careful about proposing the same design. Let‘s take an example.

Family – B:-

- Here, the husband and wife have a cooking maid.
- The tuition classes for the child are given at home, he studies himself. Now see the difference.

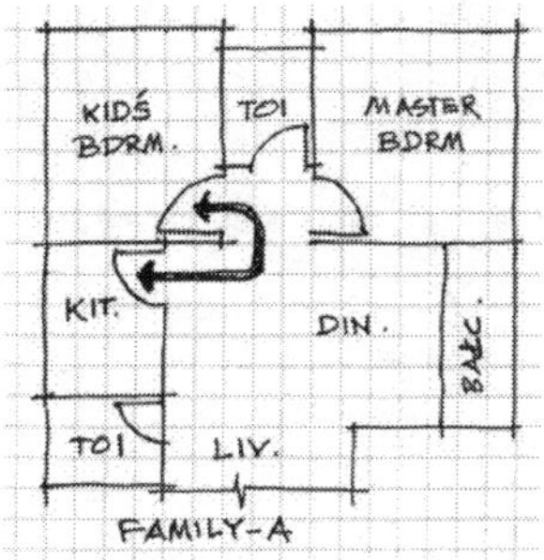

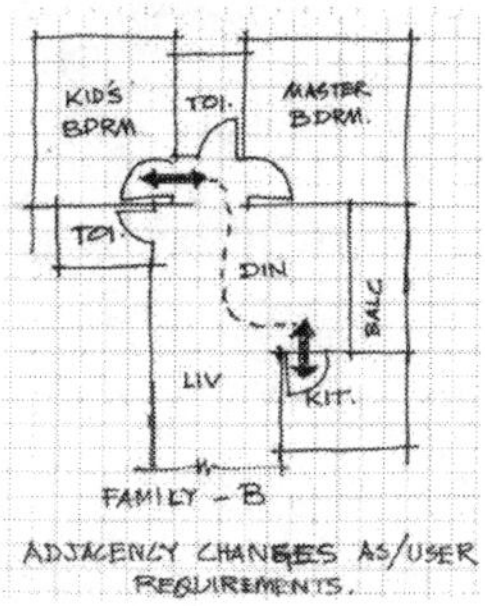

- Plan Activity before Space planning.

Let us take the example of a single bedroom now. Find out the answers to your questions like what are the activities that are going to take place in this room.

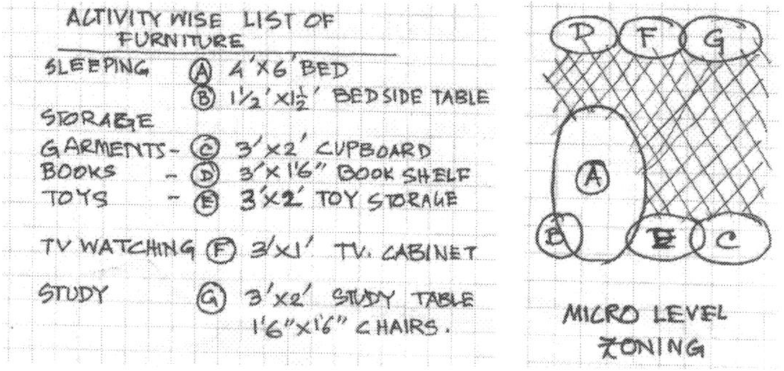

Now how to place all the furniture? Here are Eight rules for placing furniture or planning the space effectively:

While planning the space for a particular room, once you have finished collecting and jotting down details of all the activities, necessary furniture, their structural and functional dimensions and also the required circulation space, you can start putting them on a layout. While doing space planning for a particular room, once the mirror level zoning has been done, you can follow the following thumb rules to place them correctly.

1. Start planning furniture against a wall center or two walls corner.

2. Place heavy (high, wide and deep) furniture along the walls and never place them in the middle of the room.

3. While placing furniture avoid wasting corner places, space more than 1'6" to 2' can have an additional feature like the bookshelf, planter, display, etc.
4. While placing furniture, consider their functional dimension and not the structural dimension.
5. Plan for circulation space in addition to the furniture.
6. Keep the circulation flexible to accommodate access to the doors from the room.
7. 3' to 4' is maximum circulation, anything more than that without any purpose is wastage.
8. Emphasis on special collection furniture or specially design furniture to be placed to highlight.

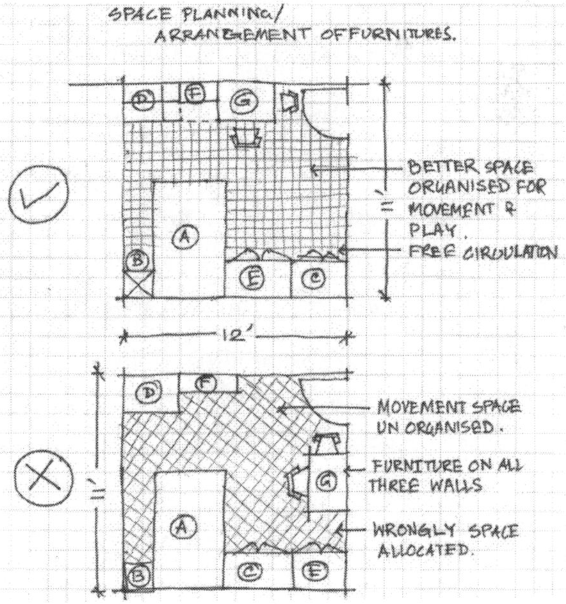

While finalizing consider Life of Design (Design durability)

Design durability is the major factor in the design decision process. Whether you are designing a residential place or commercial place, in both cases it's important to consider life design and place accordingly. Like in a city or town the space is always designed considering the future for the coming 50-100 years. Similarly in an interior project, you have to think about such factors. For residential its more guided by our socio-economic evolutions as well as the user group for whom you are designing. For each project, you need to answer three questions to make the decision regarding the life of that design.

1. What is the age group of the user at present?
2. How long they are going to stay in that residence?
3. And what is their estimation for their present proposed design to sustain?

Example – Let's say there is a family with 2 kids of 5 and 10 years at present. After 5 years they might not require a bunk bed when they grow up to 10 and 15. In the second case, they may be planning to shift to a bigger house or bungalow in the next ten years. And in the 3rd case, your client may be expecting the design to last for 20 years. Now based on these three considerations, how do your design decision changes look like?

1. You may suggest to them, instead of a bunkbed, two single beds but with a provision for sliding one under another to save place dining day time.

2. You can suggest your client to have more movable furniture than fixed one so that they can take with them

3. You need to visualize how the habit, desire and practices of the user group change in 20 years. Place the quality of materials should be able to sustain for another 20 years.

Level of comfort (Anthropometry)

Though as the beauty of materials is not exactly proportionate to the cost of the project, a similar look and feel can be achieved by opting for materials having different pricing on the budget.

However, the level of comfort is directionally proportionate to the budget of the project. Here I am going to discuss a short comparison to help you understand the same. Let's say there is a doctor in your neighborhood who charges Rs. 100 as the consultation fee. Now, the waiting area of this doctor will be different from the one who sits in a multispecialty hospital and charged Rs.1000/- per visit.

Similarly, Metro and Airport are having a different comfort quotient which gives you a clear understanding of what you paid for the services. In the case of residential spaces, cost is not the one and only guiding factor. Here the user's choice and availability of space also affect the comfort level. For example, the sofa seat can be sleek – 18"x18" or medium 21"x21" or standard 24"x24", as well as lavish or luxurious 2'x2'6" deep. Based on 1. Available space, 2. Client's requirements and 3.

Cost or budget you decide which one to opt for and accordingly you must design the level of comfort for your client, his family and guest. For each area, you have to think in a similar way and explain to your client accordingly. This is what can help significantly you in your design Decision Process.

Sustainability

Sustainability of a design is very close to the life of design but not exactly the same. In the life of design, you are designing about duration only but here you have to consider the availability of materials, durability, and maintenance and afterlife of the same. You should always select those materials that are easily available, incur less acquisition cost, which has reasonable installation cost, are functional, natural, durable and usable as well as re-usable. Lots of designers think that placing something odd in some odd place in their signature style. My recommendation is to re-think and consider all these above points before any interior design installation or during the design decision process.

Science vs. Belief

Whatever topics I am discussing here are equivalent to one complete subject. However, as I am trying to make this book easy to follow and easy to apply, so I am not going into very much detail on the subject belief of your client. Believe it or not but I have personally checked that 60-70% of our design decision can be matched with the Vaastu. So I am unrolling to you a ready decision chart to bolster you in deciding the location, orientation, direction etc. This will help you to decide your design according to Vaastu. Here it is.

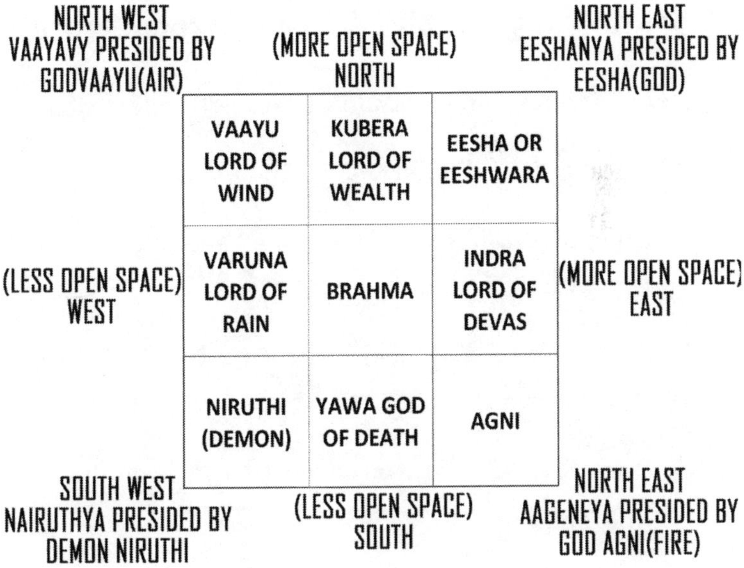

DIRECTIONS & THEIR PRESIDING DEITY

NORTH WEST VAAYAVYA		NORTH		NORTH EAST EESHANYA
	CHILDREN'S ROOM TOILET	TREASURY	ENTRANCE POOJA, MEDITATION ROOM	
WEST	DINING ROOM, STUDY ROOM	OPEN SPACE, LIVING ROOM.	TOILET, KITCHEN, STORE	EAST
	MASTER'S BEDROOM, DRESSING RM, TOOL ROOM	BEDROOM	KITCHEN	
SOUTH WEST NAIRUTHYA		SOUTH		SOUTH EAST AAGHNYA

24-point Ready checklist for Vaastu compliences

1. Doors of each room should be facing the East.

2. Bedrooms should be in the South and West.

3. Placement of mirrors on the South and West wall are inauspicious.

4. While sleeping, the head should be in the South or West but never in the North.

5. Pooja room should be in the North-East. All idols and photographs should be facing East or West.

6. The toilet seat should be in North-South only. It should not be in East-West.

7. Outhouses should not touch the compound wall of the North and Eastside.
8. Stairs should always be in a clockwise direction.
9. Anything underground should be in the North or East.
10. Anything above the ground should be in the South or West.
11. The porch should not touch the North or East compound wall.
12. Big trees should not be grown in the North or East. They should be in the South or West side of the house.
13. Face the East or North while reading or transacting any business deal.
14. Face the East while cooking, West is allowed if there is no alternative, but never face the South while cooking.
15. The total number of doors and windows should be in even number for each floor, but should not end in zero like 10, 20, 30. The width of the door should be half the height of the door. The door should not be too high, too low, too wide or too narrow. The doors should be rectangular and square doors should always be avoided.
16. Ventilation should be looked after and there should be good cross ventilation.

17. Never put the poster of crying girl, war scene, sexy scenes, angry man, owl, eagle, etc.: they are inauspicious.

18. Doors should open inside the room and not outside.

19. In bedrooms, always use a bed with four legs only. Never use box-type beds because it stops the air circulation under the bed which is bad for health.

20. Never eat or drink in a standing position.

21. No room should be built under the stairs.

22. The cupboard in the wall should be in the Southern or Western direction of the house.

23. In the kitchen, grinder, fridge, shelf and other heavy items should be towards the South and West wall.

24. There should be no water body in front of any entrance door of the house.

STEP 6

Be Methodical

Go By Strategy

In this chapter, I will show you, without going into very much technicalities, how you can progressively reach your design goal to meet the client's requirement. The challenge is that each and every project has its own unique character and needs special attention. If we have to give attention to multiple projects at a time there is a chance to miss out on some crucial points. To overcome this problem, I have developed a Design development method by using my 22 years of experience. This method has been tested for different projects irrespective of their character. It acts like a full-proof method to approach and reach concrete design solutions step-by-step without missing the minute details.

The steps can be broadly categorized into 3 stages: Data Collection, Data Analysis and Data Synthesis.

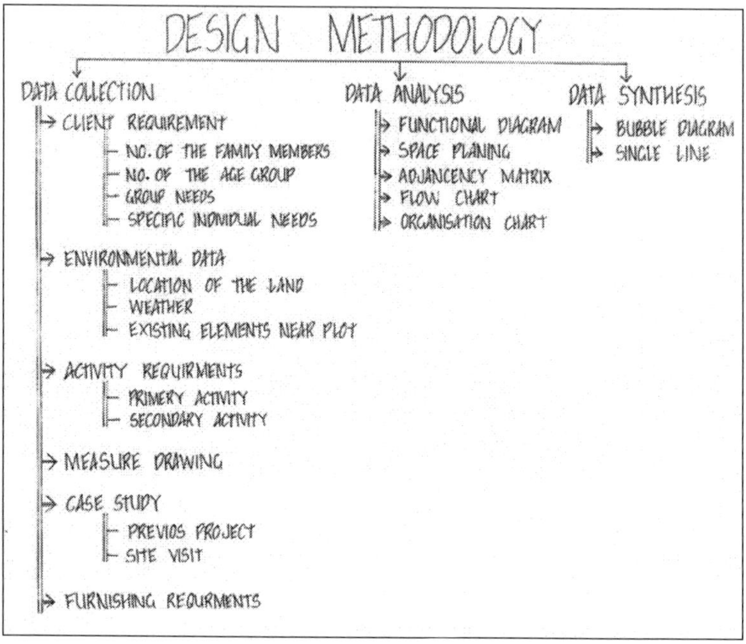

Design Approach:- Talk to your first client, that is you, start with your house/flat. Ask yourself about three things. First, what is your need, then what do you "want" and lastly your desire.

Various types of problems have different design approaches.

1. You can suggest one family about their required space and layout and can find out their exact needs accordingly. Your client can buy a space with specific numbers of rooms, toilets, etc. This way, you will have maximum space in these types of projects.

2. Someone can purchase a space with or without an exterior wall and without any interior wall. Few structural columns are there. You need to suggest the possible layouts and the best one to go with. In this case, still, the designers have a quite good scope for the suggested design.

3. The third category is addition, alteration and renovation. Your client is having a selected space with all the enclosures like external and internal walls with few possibilities to modify the layout plan or reorienting spaces, etc. Here still you have some scope with civil work i.e. shifting of the wall, dismantling or re-constructing countertops, doors, windows, spaces etc. Additional care needs to be taken for the existing services like flooring, plumbing, electrical, etc. Maximum challenges lie in this category. Most of the real-life projects come under this or the 4th category.

4. This fourth category includes a flat, residence or space with all rooms and walls. Here you can't do so much with the layout but you can work on the furniture arrangement, special elements and effects by using various materials, furnishings, etc. All needs to be applied with utmost care.

Here we shall talk about a hypothetical project where maximum scope related to the required space can be calculated. For more practice, you need to ask the following questions to yourself or later to your clients too.

1. The number of users in the project and their individual age, physical dimension or height, etc.
2. The activities they normally do based on their age.
3. Religion, culture and practices.
4. The profession of each member.
5. Any specific choice of color collections or artifacts to be displayed.
6. Space needs to be created for any specific purpose.
7. Any special hobbies like dancing, singing, book reading, sports, photography, painting, etc.
8. Any sample project photographs or references in mind.

Among the above-mentioned points. the first three points will give you an idea about your "need". The answer to query no. 4, 5, 6 & 7 will give you the list of "want" and point no. 8 will give you an idea about their desireness.

You have to address all of the above and satisfy most of them one by one.

Respect Client's Need And Desire

While you are handling any client, please show respect towards their need and desire. You can take it as their demand too. Most of the designers say that as they are an expert in their field they are already aware of the client's need and desire and this is where things go wrong.

To do effective space planning, you need to plan the Activity before you start, know how to plot those Activities in Design charts. Zoning (Macro & Micro) helps in organizing spaces with functionality; Weightage helps to reach the finest possibilities of space utilization.

Here are some charts that you can create as a part of your design process. Plot Activities in Design charts. See how a design chart should look like:

User group and activity-wise flow chart-

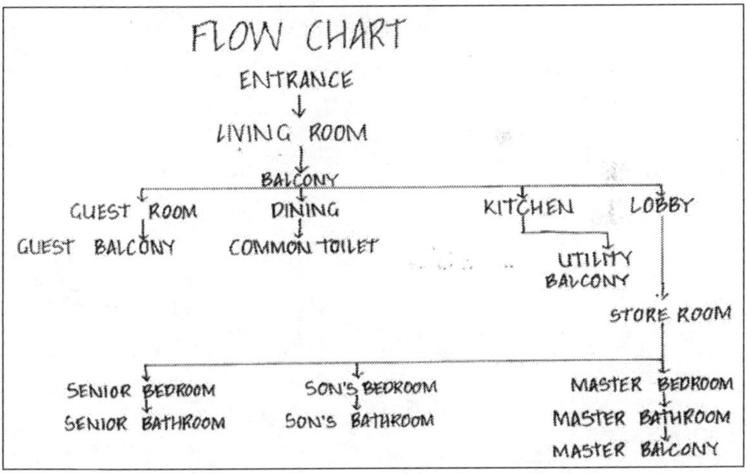

Another way to get a systematic organization chart in a residence is by considering the activity related to privacy. For example:

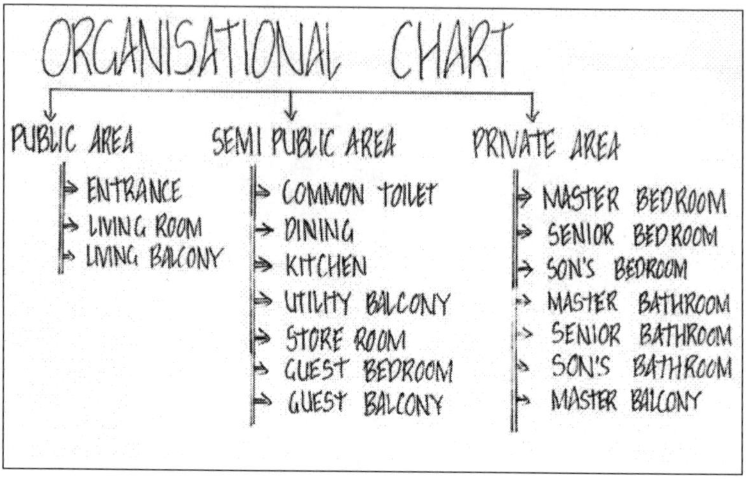

Both ways you can get a clear idea about the flow of activities within a house. So now you can start planning for the adjacency of different spaces. This step helps you to decide where to locate what facilities within a house.

In a broader spectrum, you can find out the relationship between two or more spaces. Now try the following:

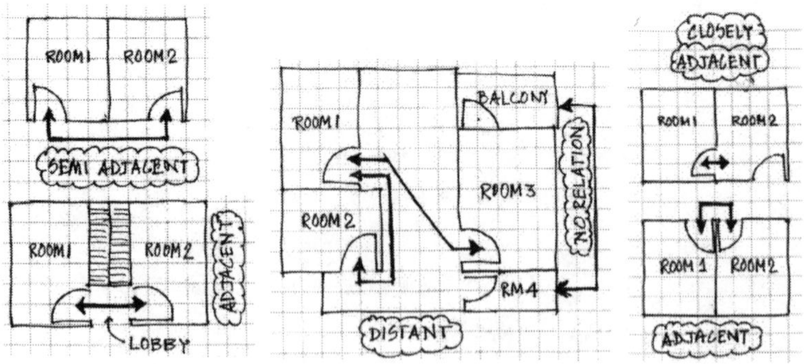

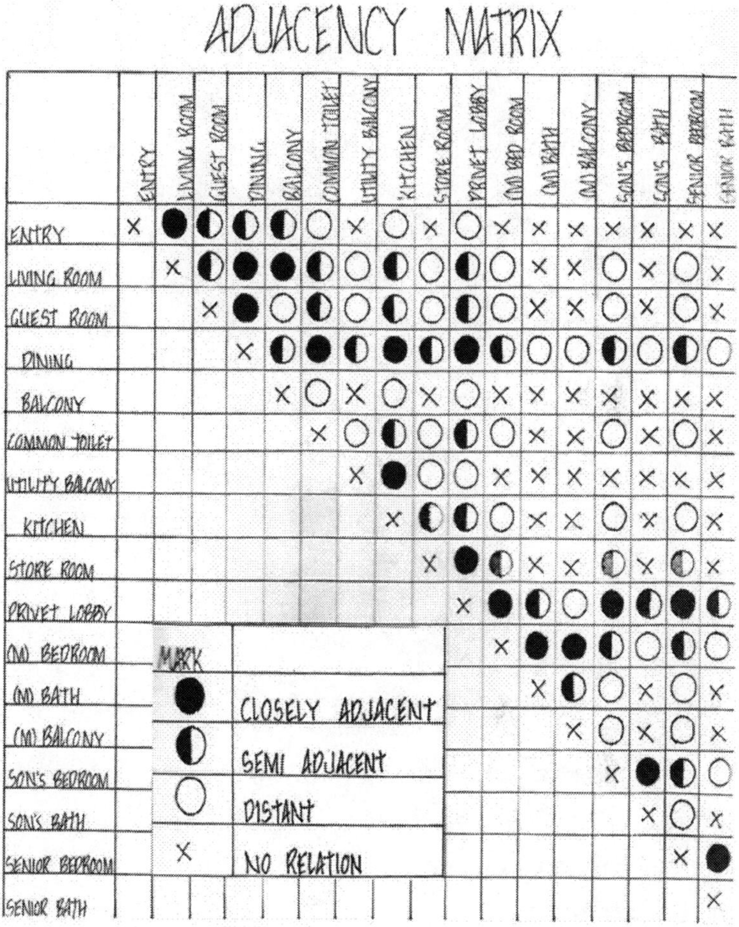

This is known as Matrix. Matrix is used for easy decision-making without any mistake. The term Matrix may be known to almost all of you, so here we are discussing about the adjacency matrix. This matrix will guide you on the relationship between any two areas with direct, indirect or no accessibility. Now there are 4 kinds of relationships between any two areas which will reflect in your Legend. Either two activities should be performed very close to each other i.e., Closely or Fully adjacent (Cooking and Dining), or can be performed near by-semi adjacent (Study and sleeping), Or maybe the activities need to be performed far away from each other (Music and study) - Distant. The last one may be those two activities that do not have any relation between them, which is also called no-relation (Master balcony and Son's study).

This is actually a thought process that you need to follow before you finalize the positions, orientation, accessibility and flow of functions.

Zoning (Macro & Micro), Weightage

The next step of design data analysis is Zoning. According to the matrix above, you need to place all the activity areas and give them positive or negative weightage functionally in more than one alternative. The maximum the points, the closer you are to the best design solution.

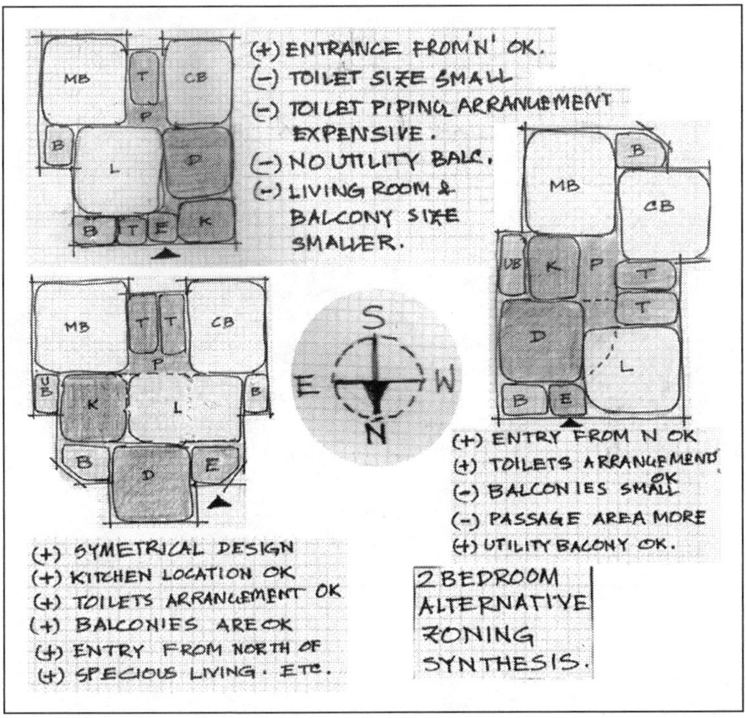

Once final zoning has been done, now you can reach to a single line diagram easily from this.

STEP 7

Be Material-Istic (Knowledge Of Materials)

Have you ever thought of doing an interior decoration without having the knowledge of different kinds of materials? It is impossible. So even after knowing the technical drawing, visualizing in 3D, collecting inspiration and following the design methods you must go by a strategy. If you are unable to propose the appropriate materials to appropriate usage, you will not be called for the second time to do a project.

So you have to be prepared with these kinds of queries.

- What are the traditional or conventional materials needed in Interior Design or to construct and decorate the interior?

- What is the difference between unconventional materials and newer materials that come into the market?

At the same time, it might be difficult to know everything about each material available in the market. So here in this chapter, I will suggest how to manage the material applications properly in any interior design project.

You just need to remember two things here, 1st one is the elements and the 2nd one is the name of some companies that supply different kinds of materials. These elements which I am talking about are not those elements that you have studied in chapter one as design elements. These are the Interior elements. The major elements where you need to apply materials are floor, wall and ceiling; few more elements are doors, windows, staircase railings, balcony railings, furniture, arches/lintels, furnishings, etc.

Interior Design is basically designing the envelope which is majorly covered by three things as I mentioned floor, wall and ceiling. We have some natural and some manmade products.

- Natural or Manmade stones or Mosaic or Granular finish
- Stones like Quartz, Granite, Indian marble, imported marble, other stones
- Tiles (verified, rectified, ceramic, concrete, etc.)

- Wooden (laminate, ply or solid wood plunk)
- Synthetic materials (rubber, cork, nylon, etc.)
- Glass as an exceptional material
- PVC material
- Gypsum POP
- Fabrics & Carpets
- Metals
- Any composite materials
- Epoxy or any kind of paint

As I have promised you to help you learn Interior Design to start your business immediately, so if I start giving you more details on different kinds of flooring materials and their specification or usage, it may take more time. Rather, I would like to show you the way how you can handle your client with the application of various materials on different Interior Design elements. If you wish to study more on this you are welcome to my educational portal. If you canot then the best way is visiting the market. Go to a vendor who sells marble or different kinds of stones, he will guide you about the thickness, designs, application, fixing, process, etc. If your design is inspired by wooden flooring, do a little bit of hard work on the internet as well as visit your nearest shop that sells wooden flooring. There you can feel the look, design and can also know more about the application method and specifications. Though I am suggesting you to sink your teeth in the market survey, yet, I am also attaching a reckoner for the beginners. You can refer to this reckoner for different kinds of materials and their usage.

You have to understand the philosophy and logic behind the application of each material. So if you are suggesting a floor for the living room, you should suggest the best one as it shows the taste of the family who lives there. Even you have a lesser budget for the floor, you can have a mix and match of costly and less costly materials and use in this sequence.

The best one - medium one - effective one - the lowest priced one shall be arranged in the living room - bedroom - toilet & kitchen - balconies or internal lobbies in series. It should be organized in a way that the average price of flooring fits into your client's budget.

The choice of flooring material also depends on the frequency and number of users using the same. The durability of material largely depends on this factor.

Another guiding factor to choose a perfect floor is maintenance. You can ask your client about the pattern and system of cleaning they follow at their home and accordingly you can suggest the flooring material.

One more factor that applies to any material is the quality and specification. The same kind of looks with a different kind of thickness or gauge and specification are available in the market. So it is always recommended to go by the client's budget while choosing materials.

Here I am sharing some Traditional and some unconventional materials for your detailed knowledge.

Conventional or Traditional Materials

Let me tell you one thing, most of the books, journals or write up will ask you to first study a few names, their characters, specification, etc. for different materials without understanding their application or leaving you to experiment on those. Here, I am suggesting you a different method altogether. In the beginning of this book, the first step that I recommend is to be passionate and imperial. You have learned to create the inspiration board based on your design strategy in the last chapter. Now you start searching for suitable materials for each element that you have incorporated in your design. This is where you can apply your creative skills.

For all kinds of traditional on conventional materials like brick, stone, timber, glass, PVC, etc. if you study in this sequence, it will be easier for you to apply the same properly. Each element of your design envelop that is floor, wall, and ceiling having two basic stages to create. One is the construction and the other one is finishing or appearances. So, almost all the traditional materials are available for these two purposes in the market. Eg.

brick is available for content walls (External 230 – 250 mm and internal 115 – 125 mm) depending upon the local standards and availability. At the same time, if you want a look and feel of the brick exposed to give special effects, you will get it in the form of cladding on the wall in various thicknesses and designs. And definitely, when it is used as a cladding on a vertical surface, it will be of higher weight and thinner width. Now think about Timber. When we use timber for creating the structure of a wall, we use a harder and solid wood. At the same time, to cover those, we use ply (6mm, 12mm, 19mm, 125mm and in between some other thicknesses are available in the market). And to have a look and finish of timber, we use veneer and polish or laminates of lesser thickness like .6mm, .8mm, 1mm or 1.5mm, etc. or think about Stone. To construct a wall, we use thinner slabs. On the floor, if slabs are available in 16mm, 19mm, 20mm thickness for the wall, we may go for a thinner slab respecting the law of gravity and ease of binding. The same is applicable for glass. Glass blocks or glass bricks are used to construct an interior wall for a special look with more transparency than a brick, stone or timber partition wall. At the same time, the glass sheet in 4mm, 5mm, 6mm, 8mm, 10mm can give the look and feel on the floor, wall or ceiling.

I have not discussed few of the materials here to make my book short, crispy and to restrict time to read it. But trust me, the way I am telling you is going to make you a teacher for yourself. Whenever you see new materials in the market, try to visualize like this, whether you are going to use it for the construction of elements or to get the look and feel of the same elements upon completion.

Once you have become an expert on the purpose of each material, you can try the non-conventional materials or use regular materials in a non-conventional way or buy fusion application of both. You can use conventional and traditional materials with an unconventional or newer one. Here I have mentioned a few for your reference.

1. Brick:-

Brick is used in flooring, decorative half-walls, and entryways to make grand entrances into a home. There are two types of bricks available in the market traditional (made from mud/earth) and nontraditional (made of different kinds of material like fly ash, concrete mix, etc.) These are known as modular bricks.

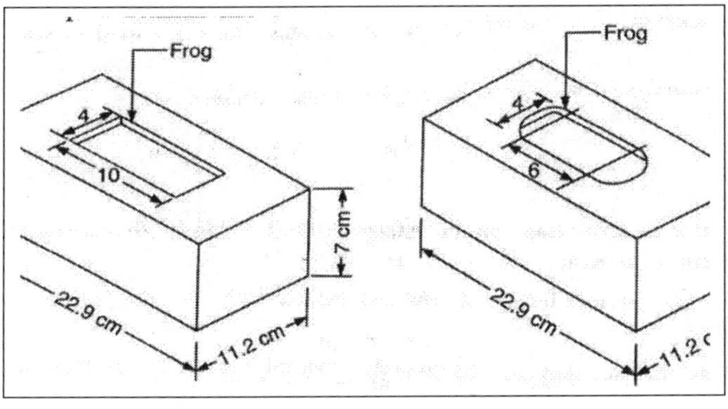

Fig. 1

The three different available qualities are 1st class, 2nd class and 3rd class bricks. Normally the degree of burning, accuracy of sizes and neatness of edges vary in these three classes. Usage of these is also different. The third class of bricks is used for roads, second class for walls and the first class for exposed walls.

2. Tile:

This is a manufactured piece of hard-wearing material such as ceramic, stone, metal, baked clay, or even glass, generally used for covering roofs, floors, walls, or other objects such as tabletops.

3. Stone:

Natural stones are luxurious eco-friendly materials for modern interior design and decorating. Stone slabs, stone tile designs, mosaics, modern furniture and lighting fixtures made with a natural stone look spectacular and amazing, blending the elegant style into living spaces and office designs.

Chic marble, durable granite, spectacular onyx, gorgeous quartz, warm travertine, practical slate and limestone work great as flooring ideas and wall decoration materials. Semi-precious and precious stones give a fabulous look to the modern interior design and are preferred for decorating in any style.

Marble stone slabs are classic materials for interior design and decor. Granite, onyx and travertine slabs have their own character which enriches the modern interior design or emphasizes classic style decorating. Marble and onyx are the most luxurious choices which create a fascinating, expensive and unique look.

Some types of natural stones create wonderful additional visual effects. Colorful onyx has a translucent texture and can be combined with modern lighting fixtures for a soft glowing effect. This

natural stone is very decorative and can turn an accent wall into a spectacular artwork.

Stone tiles in square, rectangular, triangular, and hexagonal shapes or free shaped tile designs are popular trends in decorating and interior design. Stone tiles are perfect for flooring ideas, bathroom and kitchen backsplash ideas and excellent, spectacular and stylish wall design materials.

Stone mosaic tiles are one of the ancient interior designs and decorating materials that are still stylish and popular. Pebbles and small stones, or sophisticated mosaic tile designs create unique floor and wall decorations, celebrating the natural materials and creativity of artistic mind.

The beauty of natural marble-like onyx or travertine influences creative and unique furniture design. Stone coffee tables, chairs, dining tables, shelves, console tables and nightstands perfectly combine the natural stone with wood and metal, creating a modern furniture design that fits into modern home interiors

4. Terrazzo, Similar Composites, and Concrete

Terrazzo is a composite material, poured in place or precast, which is used for floor and wall treatments. It consists of chips of marble, quartz, granite, glass, or other suitable material, poured with a cementitious binder (for chemical binding), polymeric (for physical binding), or a combination of both.

Polished concrete contains more **cement** whereas **terrazzo** contains more aggregate. **Polished concrete** involves **polishing** the slab. In contrast, **terrazzo** involves covering the **concrete** slab with epoxy and aggregate, and then grind and **polished** to a finish. Terrazzo can have multiple color schemes based on the chips used as an aggregate.

5. Wood:

Wood is the most loved material for Interior design. It is used in flooring, walls, paneling or for vertical separation as partition or woodworks, furniture, door, window, staircase, ceiling, lighting as well as artifacts and any other decorations. Woods are available in three forms like plunk, slab and laminate. Slab can be natural or created artificially with various composite layers called ply and block boards available in various thicknesses. To get a wooden finish veneer and laminates are available in the market. Veneer needs to be polished whereas laminates come as a finished product and have to be pasted on the ply surface.

6. Plastic:

Though in the present scenario plastic is the most harmful material for the ecosystem of planet Earth, yet few composite materials made of plastic are still being used in interior decoration. Areas like bathroom, kitchen and wet areas require some amount of plastic materials as protection against water. The durability of **plastics** makes them ideal for **applications** such as window frames and pipes. **Plastics** provide effective insulation from cold and heat, prevent energy leakage, and allow households to save energy while also reducing noise pollution. **Plastics** with two-dimensional molecular structures are termed thermoplastics and can be heat softened and recycled. Two thermoplastics commonly **used** in the **furniture** industry are polypropylene (Robin Day's poly chair) and eco-questionable PVC (polyvinyl chloride), **used** for panel edging and foils.

Charcoal Sheets are made from 100% recycled plastics, covered in unconventional material.

7. *Glass:*

Interior designing can never be made much stylish and elegant without **glass usage.** As **glass** provides all the possible ways to decorate your home furniture, there's a wide range of glass available for interiors that too in different textures and patterns. It can be transparent, translucent or opaque!

These are termed as the:

- **Clear Glass:** The glass that provides a clear view of both outside as well as inside.
- **Tinted Glass:** They are light-colored glasses. Hence, depending upon the tinting, the direct glare of sunlight can be dimmed or reduced.
- **Frosted Glass:** It blurs out the images but still transmits light. Therefore, this is a glass used for visual privacy.
- **Reflective Glass:** This type of glass has a mirror-like coating on its exterior surface. It reflects heat and radiation from sunlight but still allows the natural light to come in. Safety-wise the three main types of processed glass are:
- **Toughened Glass:** It is up to five times stronger than ordinary glass. If it breaks, it will shatter into small pieces without any sharp edges hence, potential cuts and

injuries can be avoided. It even facilitates easier cleanup as one does not have to carefully pick up the sharp pieces.

Tempered Glass and Toughened Glass are almost the same and the terms are used interchangeably. These are extremely durable and ten times stronger than regular glass. Even these glasses reduce the chances of injury that is caused by shattering. Moreover, tempered glass is significantly cheaper when compared to laminated glass.

- **Laminated Glass:** Laminated glass consists of two or more glass permanently bonded together with one or multiple layers of polyvinyl butyral (PVB). It is used when safety is paramount. As when broken, it prevents the glass from fragmenting and is held in place by the interlayer. Though it produces a cracking pattern but keeps the layers of glasses bonded. It's the same glass that is used in car windscreens, walk on floors, shower cubicles and so on. It is even used for sound insulation and can also withstand drastic changes in temperatures.

8. *Metals:*

In interiors, the presence of metal can add beauty, strength, austerity, solidity and sophistication to the scheme. The level of each will be determined by the kind of metal and how it is used.

Here are seven of the designer‘s favorites (3 alloys and 4 pure metals):

Brass

An alloy, the combination of copper and zinc, it has a distinctive yellow color. One of its most popular uses is for decorative surfaces, furniture and in the lighting industry. Brass is also used as the divider of floors that gives an effect of golden line on marble or granite floor.

Iron

Iron is a very strong material, used commonly in the building industry. It was used extensively in the Victorian times and Art Noveau as wrought iron, from which extraordinary pieces of intricate design were made. Nowadays wrought iron is very famous in making furniture like bed, sofa and artifacts too.

Bronze

Another alloy product of copper and tin, it has become one of the favorite materials for furniture, paneling and architectural elements like balustrades, windows, handrails, etc. Its brownish color offers that discreet elegance so sought after in some contemporary interiors. Its higher cost makes it popular for high-end projects.

Aluminium

A soft metal, it has been used predominantly for doors and windows. Thanks to its susceptibility to chemical reactions, it can acquire different and long-lasting colors (from the anodizing process). There are other processes that allow the aluminum to have a copper, brass, stainless steel and even a chrome look at a less expensive price than the original ones.

Due to its fantastic anti-corrosive qualities, mosaics and tiling are produced as well. Aluminium is used as the framing material to false ceiling and as exposed liner ceiling too.

Steel

Steel is an alloy that depending on the combination of iron and carbon plus other ingredients, can take the form of stainless steel or corten iron; both completely different in look and feel. Stainless steel has been used widely in interiors for surfaces, kitchens‘ splashback, balustrades, etc. It is a product very easy to clean and maintain. Its look has been associated with a modern look.

When in corten form, it takes on a beautiful rusty patina that can be manipulated following chemical or natural intervention to produce a surface rich in texture and color (brown-red-orange). Steel as metal in interior also comes under un-conventional usage in various cases.

Copper

It has been used with a certain discretion so far in interiors, mostly in decorative schemes. Its red- pink color is very distinctive which forces one to be very accurate in the proportioning of it as it can overwhelm easily; great for furniture, ironmongery and decorative surfaces.

Nickel

It is similar to stainless steel but with a grade of yellow in it which makes it warmer and more elegant in appearance. Used mostly in ironmongery, handles and accessories. It is a finish that will definitely enhance the look of any interior. Wood and leather are great complements for their particular beauty.

9. Paints, Coatings, and Wallcovering

Wallcoverings refer to anything you use to design and decorate your walls from wallpaper and paint to more creative materials like plaster or decorative fabrics. Your wall coverings choice depends on the room function, your interior design vision, practical questions like maintenance, ease of installation, and even your ability to change your wall covering or it's color.

Modern interior design trends in wall coverings include nature-inspired wall coverings created with digital photo prints, unique wallpaper patterns that mimic wood, brick or concrete, carved wood wall paneling, floral wallpaper patterns, geometric or striped wallpaper designs, natural materials and luxurious wall panels with 3d designs, textured wall tiles and chic wall covering fabrics.

Interior paint comes in five types of finish. There's the gloss paint which is great for kitchens and bathrooms, semi-gloss paint which is durable but less shiny, satin paint which has a low shine and is easy to clean, eggshell paint that has a barely discernable gloss and flat paint which has almost no reflective quality.

Lighting is very important when choosing the color and type of paint. It's important to look at the color swatches during the day and during the night and to take into consideration the lighting that you have in your home.

10. Textiles, Window Treatments and Soft Goods

Textiles, frequently referred to as soft furnishings, are fabrics used in the home. They include items frequently classified as linens, such as bath and dish towels, table linens, shower curtains, and bathroom ensembles. Related items include sheets, pillowcases, mattresses, blankets, comforters, and bedspreads.

Fabric, one can say, might be the most underrated element in interior design; since one normally tends to think of furniture, lighting, etc. Fabric is in fact, one of the core elements of interior design. Fabric adds colors to the interior, whether home or office. The colors can vary according to the place – bright, warm colors for homes and dark, subtle hues for offices. Fabric color should be chosen in accordance with the furniture since the blend of those two adds to the overall effect the theme of the interior suggests. Normally offices go for plain, solid-colored fabrics whereas one can expect fabrics of different patterns and designs for homes. The designs can vary from traditional, embroidery, cross-stitch, etc.

11. Carpeting and Area Rugs

Be it in the living room, bedroom or dining room, area rugs feel right at home. As a rule of thumb; use an area rug under the largest piece, or group of furniture, in a room to anchor the space and absorb sound. Especially when accompanied by an ample rug pad, area rugs do a wonderful job of buffering noise

Rugs have the ability to complement a room and give it a smoother, unified look with respect to colors.

Rug gives an alternative feeling of changed texture than other smooth surfaces. A fine rug can create a very tranquil atmosphere whilst chunky carpets can lend a sense of comfort and warmth

12. Resilient Flooring

Resilient flooring, also called vinyl flooring is a flooring created from carefully selected natural and synthetic materials. This product construction has changed over the years, just as products in other industries have incorporated new and better technology, resilient flooring has as well. The material that binds the mixture together is either asphalt (asphaltum) or resin. There are six main types of resilient flooring: linoleum, asphalt, vinyl (composition and solid), rubber, wood and cork. Roll flooring comes in the form of large sheets of material. Few of these are described under unconventional materials as well.

Of special importance in areas with heavy floor traffic. Resilient flooring, in general, will cushion impacts and thereby reduce traffic noise or noise from dropped objects more than other hard- surface floors such as wood, marble, ceramic or concrete.

13. Laminated Materials and Substrates

Laminates are artificially produced material from paper and resins. They are quite popularly known as sunmica. Such decorative laminates are fixed on substrate as a finishing layer for MDF, plywood, particleboard, wooden furniture, wall panels and flooring. A composite artificial material, they are made by pressing together thin layers of flat paper and plastic resins. The upper layer is printed with a decorative pattern or color and available in various thicknesses like .6mm, .8mm. 1mm & 1.25mm.

Un-Conventional or Non-Traditional Materials

Woven resin

It is meant to look like natural wicker but is made of synthetic material, generally polyethylene. Synthetic polyethylene fiber resin wicker is generally durable, resistant to the sun's UV radiation and water. Resin wicker is often used over an aluminum frame to create lightweight outdoor furniture.

Three-D gypsum board

Fiberglass-reinforced gypsum board panels come in tiles and are screwed to a substrate. The seams are mudded and sanded by a skillful dry-waller to create a continuous effect.

Faux leather

This leather look-alike rubber product has a beautiful tactile warmth and is available in three different hues: Natural, chocolate (shown here) and black.

Faux leather is very durable and will last a long time. It can withstand scratches and scrapes that would mar genuine leather. It is not prone to crack or peel like leather.

Since it‘s a rubber product, it‘s easy to maintain and suitable for kitchen and bathroom cabinetry.

Stainless steel

Steel has amazing potential and can take on many different personalities, from modern and stark to tactile and warm.

Stainless steel isn't used just as a sheet metal today. In new applications, stainless steel pieces are linked together like chain mail or woven into screens.

Laminated glass

Laminated glass is made of various flat products sandwiched between two sheets of glass; it has a high-end, pressed look.

Colored glass works beautifully with this application, too. Mirror can be used as a backing for an opaque, reflective insert in a closet door. You can try playing with frosted glass, Starphire glass or different fabric inlays.

Laminated resin

Polyester laminating resin, also known as fiberglass resin, is the most commonly used resin in the industry. It is used in a wide variety of projects including boats, car bodies, kayaks, surfboards, patio decks and aircraft. It is affordable and easy to use. It has a quick cure and adds dimensional stability.

Laminated resin is often used as a cabinet door inserts or for lamp shades, but it can also be applied on a larger scale. The skillful mix of laminated resin in this photo gives a workspace the calm quality of a Japanese tearoom.

Woven vinyl

Woven vinyl (sometimes also called woven PVC) is a unique flooring material. It is woven from textile polyester yarn coated with a heavy-duty vinyl layer. Although it's marketed as a commercial- grade product, woven vinyl would make for great low-maintenance headboards or kitchen banquette upholstery.

Cinder Blocks

Cinder block is fabricated of- concrete and coal cinders. Concrete block is produced by steel, wood, and cement. A concrete block contains stone or sand which makes it heavier. Cinder blocks don't have any tensile strength to withstand pressure.

Poured and paneled concrete might be the more obvious choices, but everyday cinder blocks can also lend a sophisticated industrial effect to walls and floors.

Acoustic Tiles

Prized primarily for their ability to absorb and remit sound, acoustic tiles are also kind of mod and cool-looking. The team at Float Studio—the go-to designers for start-ups seeking sophisticated office space on a budget has used it to panel the walls of a few in-office telephone booths, left unpainted for visual impact.

Copper Pipes

While typically pricier than less flashy pipe materials, copper piping still isn't an exorbitant purchase for small projects. Once armed with enough of it, you can cut it using this eentsy, easy-to-use device and screw together hanging utensil racks, side tables, even faucets.

Wax

For a watery-but-protective finish over any construction-grade plaster, try using wax the way Neal Beckstedt did over the massive, undulating black hearth in his room at the 2017 Kips Bay Showhouse. No paint will get you a glimmering look like that.

Cork

Not just for framing and covering with ribbons from your teenager's swim meets, cork sheets can also be used to add a visually textural surface on floors and walls.

Steel Sheets

Available in a wide array of gauges and finishes, steel sheets can be fashioned into doors, table toppers, walls, and the like.

Peg Board

While perhaps an obvious choice for organizational purposes in, say, the kitchen, a pegboard wall can also be used just to add an unexpected touch (especially when painted an edgy color) to other walls. Oversized is especially fun.

Charcoal board

Charcoal Decorative Sheet for Interior. Charcoal sheet is you can say a type of laminate but, it is not exactly a laminate. It is a PVC based material for decorating purposes. Charcoal sheet is a quite simple and effective material for your home interior and furniture.

These products are a mixture of Charcoal and Polystyrene. Charcoal incorporates strength to the product whereas Styrofoam made from recycled thermocol (EPS and HIPS) makes the product resistant to warping.

Charcoal Sheets are made from 100% recycled plastics. These are hard, dense, moderate UV resistance and waterproof. It is used in tabletops, bathroom paneling, doors, shelving and wet rooms.

Application of Material

So far we have covered different materials applicable to the floor to decorate the wall and cover it up. We can use almost similar materials like timber, glass, PVC, stone but with a little bit change in specification. Floor is a horizontal surface that is exposed to more load and thrust, so it should have more hardness, thickness and quoting. Good quality flooring materials should be preferred. In the case of wall, we can degrade the specification by one or two levels. For example, if we are using 18- 20 mm thick marble on floor with a diamond polish, for the wall we can take the same marble in 12- 16 mm of thickness with may be hydra, leather or satin polish. Wall is good to feel and look; the floor should be comfortable to walk on. So, what I am trying to convey here is that the type of materials available in the market are same, you only need to change the specification to apply in different areas like floor, wall or ceiling.

Let us again take the example of the wood that can be used on the floor as wooden flooring or wall as a partition or paneling and as the wooden ceiling but the difference is in the specification. We might suggest wooden plank on the floor, wooden veneer or ply with laminate on walls and wooden jali or laminates pasted on thinner ply for the ceiling so that it should not fall onus. The same is applicable in the case of stone, metal, glass, PVC, etc.

The application which you need to understand is you have to complement the Floor, Wall and Ceiling; the three elements by using materials. If we use wood everywhere, it might not look appealing. But we can play with the color; dark and light or solid and grains or textured and plain, etc. For example, if we are using light color material on the floor, we can have darker furniture or wall or a part of the wall and ceiling to complement each other. Similarly, if we are using dark shades on the floor, it is recommended to put light shades of furniture, wall or furnishings.

But now, with the information shared in this chapter and with a little hard work on market availability, you are becoming an expert on material. Now, let me highlight a few more points regarding the material aspect, which are as follows:

- Always have an alternative selection for materials as it depends on the market availability and might affect your project schedule.
- Once the material board is ready and approved, immediately block the required quantity with the suppliers.
- Take 15 to 45 day's time in hand for material delivery depending upon the type of material.
- Handling the stacking of materials needs to be done very carefully to minimize breakage. Extra budget to be allotted for material transport and handling.
- Considering the wastage and breakage, always estimate 10-15% of extra quantity than the actual quantity.
- Market fashion changes very frequently so survey the market before suggesting any materials to your clients for the project.

- Material quality plays a major role in project budgeting. So, always make it very much clear to your client about the quality, specification brand or uniqueness to support your budget and to avoid any unwanted expectation from the client.

- In some cases, the client can purchase and provide the materials for execution. Make sure that you provide him a detailed schedule of material flow with quantity like cash flow as described in chapter - 9.

Once you have reached the end of this chapter, you have actually become an expert in material knowledge for interior design. However, there is no end to learning. Few materials like Brick, Stone, Glass, Timber, Paint, Metal, etc. are always in trend. Some like Terrazo, Wallpaper and other unconventional materials are used periodically, as fashion changes trends also change. Last but not least, new materials come into the market based on availability and technology. So you need to be aware of the market during all the time of your practice.

STEP 8

Be Professional

So far, you have almost completed all the technical aspects being a non-technical person. Now its time to be more professional before you step in the business. Professionalism is the best way to practice any discipline. Here in this chapter, I am going to explain the following:

- Value of professionalism
- Process of registering yourself as a practicing Interior Designer
- Types of remuneration or fee
- Types of Contracts or work order
- How to make profit from your project
- How to prepare estimation and budgeting for your client
- Why and How to write a specification

Value of Professionalism

The basic fundamental professionalism lies not in a particular field or profession but in your behavior. Therefore, you need to practice a few of them here as well like being on time, being well-dressed, being well-behaved, being true to your customer, keeping THE commitment, explaining things properly without hiding any facts and figures, value your client's time and your time as well, getting into a proper agreement before starting the project.

Wherever you have called for a meeting, whether you are on a site visit or materials vendor's showroom visit, you should always reach 2 minutes early or exactly on time irrespective of weather conditions, traffic conditions, distance from your place or job load on you. It is also not recommended to reach more than 10 – 15 minutes early or it might show that your workload is not much or it might spawn a doubt in your client's mind about your honesty regarding the material purchase or vendor selection. Being on time should be your first professional approach to your client.

Being well-dressed is the next very important aspect in each profession, especially Interior design. Let me explain why would someone rely on you to decorate their living space. If you are unable to maintain yourself, your hair, makeup, dress properly or you are unable to choose a proper dress for yourself, how would you do the same for your client's space. Makeup does not mean you have to make it loud. You need to maintain a balance between your face, hair, dress, accessories and shoes. These are the must requirements. Hair whether tied or not has to be organized. Instead of makeup, you can keep your face clean with a light sunscreen quote, liner on eyes and medium shade lipstick if you are a female and male can have a clean shaved face with organized hair.

Regarding makeup, hair and dress, I would like to share a story with you. When I migrated from Delhi to Kolkata, one day, one of my old clients called me and gave me a reference, "I am sending someone to your place, they want to buy an apartment near your place and seek a suggestion from you regarding it's Interior." I said "OK." However, they arrived before time and they didn't have much time to wait. They directly reached my home where I was in a very casual dress, wearing a sandal, my face was not done with proper makeover and hair was not organized. As they were in a hurry, they didn't agree to wait and forced me to take them to the suggested apartment beside the Ganges. It was such a beautiful place, that they immediately liked and booked it with the dealer. They also appointed me as their Architect.

During my explanation and making suggestions, they could guess my credential and they liked my ideas too. They asked me from where I had pursued my Architecture degree. I proudly told them about my engineering college which is the oldest in India (established 150 years ago), Bengal Engineering College, Shibpur. The lady surprisingly said to me, "Oh! You are from that college!

That‘s the best one in the Country, but you do not like you have passed from that college. You don‘t dress or makeup or hairdo that way!” I was shocked. Anyway, they left on that day with full satisfaction, I drafted my ideas and sent the layout to them. They sent me a packet full of remuneration for the Architectural part which was much higher than my expectation at that time.

However, they opted for a different Interior Designer from Germany. Later, I understood that my appearance did not match with their Interior Decoration look, feel and expectation. In spite of my higher degree, experience and satisfactory proposal, I had to lose my client only because of my appearance.

I remember my early days wherein my “Guru” who used to take me to various clients for different projects. He always used to carry a comb in his pocket and every time before we got down to the meeting place, he used to ask me to comb my hair. So, it is very important to be organized in your appearance as well.

Being well-behaved is another aspect of professionalism in any business especially when you are handling clients. Here also, I would like to narrate a true story. After I became a well-established Architect and Interior Designer in spite of my passion for training business, I have never compromised with my consultancy and Interior business. Recently, I was introduced to a client from a reference. We met and visited the site. In the first visit, I never talk about the entire project, so I asked him to appoint me as his consultant first and then I would discuss the budget, detailing and concept, if he likes my layout, he can give me the entire project to execute. The gentleman listened to everything very politely, he understood my experience, remuneration and we left. After a few followups and almost after two-three months, when I started believing that he will never come back and I have lost that project, suddenly one day he called, "Mrs. Sinha can we meet?" In the very first part of the meeting, he clearly mentioned the reason for the delay as follows. He said that after receiving my quotation, he approached two-three more interior designers and decided not to opt for them. He said, "One designer rejected me saying that they don't do projects in this budget, they do only those projects that are four times higher than his budget. The second designer quoted an absurd budget for my project and the third designer was parallel or a little below my remuneration. But the lady is having a DP of a beautiful lady on the social media that does match with her actual profile." Aww! My jaw dropped, I thought he was flirting with me. But believe me, he was a gentleman with a nice family. He immediately introduced me to her wife and kid. He clearly told me, "Mrs. Sinha, I feel comfortable speaking with you. You look and behave as you are, there is no hidden entity. So I am appointing you as our consultant." This evinces that people love to see your original face whether it's through social media or a one-to-one meeting. So, your behavior, language, posture matters a lot for them with whom you are communicating.

Commitment- Keeping commitment is the most important aspect of any profession. Your commitment regarding time to be present for a meeting, timely deliveries of material, drawings, commitment regarding the quality of material, quality of workmanship, commitment of proposed budget and estimation should be kept. Regarding time, you should not deviate and follow the scheduled time (explained in chapter – 9). Regarding quality, I always relate it with the budget because for the same- size project with almost the same scope, clients can have different budgets. One 3-bedroom apartment can have a budget of x amount and also 4x amount with almost similar facilities. So, in interior design, you have to handle the client from the beginning by giving alternative estimation with two/three different budgets depending upon the quality and make or brand of the material. If you keep your client aware of the quality differentiation based on their budget, your commitment regarding the same will not fail. Commitment related to the budget in interior design ought to be very much flexible. As it changes with the changing scope, so better to have proper documentation of things like quotations, bills, payments, delivery note, challan, etc.. 10 – 15% of the budget should always be kept flexible. This will help you not to fail in the commitment to the project budget.

Valuing time is another aspect of professionalism. I always take the example of a doctor offering consultancy without charging any fees which is very rare. So, my first meeting and a broad idea with a broad per square feet budget range is the only thing I share free of cost. You should also be aware of the value of your time. Whenever you feel the customer wants more from you but is paying nothing, either you invite him for a cup of tea/coffee at your place or directly tell him how much you charge for the per day for the site visit or measuring the site or per proposal or 3-dimensional views, etc. inviting client to your office for further discussion helps you in many ways to retain him. The client can have a feeling of your workspace, your human resource, your past projects as a portfolio, your credentials, certifications and affiliations. If all the samples and material catalogs are kept at your office, you can ask your client to come only to see those and decide. In the interior design profession clients visiting your place are 99% converted into customers. There is almost no risk to lose him as they only invest their time to visit your place once they are confident about you. 1% of the customers spend a lot of time rooming around the consultant's office to negotiate or find out efficiency.

The next step of professionalism that you show to your client is when you ask him to get into a proper MOU or agreement. Whether it is on a stamp paper or in your letterhead, there must be an understanding signed between you and your client. It is a must. You can prepare 2/3 different types of agreements, one for consultancy and supervision, one for Labour contract only and one for the labour and material turnkey contract. Do a little bit of modifications in those templates project-wise and use it. It will save you time.

Here I have created a mind map for you to make it easy to understand the major steps or services to add in your agreement.

1. Preliminary design
   - Furniture layout
   - List/legend for the same (Fur.+D/W)
   - Concept photographs
   - Mood board/concept board

2. Design Development-1
   - Sectional Elevation
   - Flooring Layout
   - False Ceiling Layout
   - Preliminary Estimate
   - Approved make

3. Design Development-1
   - Electrical Layout
   - Plumbing Layout
   - Kitchen Details
   - Toilet Details
   - Landscape Design*

4. Detail Drawing
   - Door/Window Detail
   - Finishing Schedule
   - Furniture Detail
   - Room/Space-wise
   - Bill of Quantities

5. Advance Services Design →
   - Fire Fighting*
   - HVAC*
   - Acoustics* Thermal
   - Insulation*
6. Materials Sourcing
7. Site Supervision
8. Project Planning and Management

The items marked with a '*' can be outsourced, but it should be clearly mentioned in the agreement that these are not under the designer's scope. The coordination between all these is a part of the designer's responsibility.

Here, I am attaching a template of headings or topics that need to be included in your contract- Annexure-XX.

Though it is very easy to jot down the points based on this template completely by yourself and as per your understanding but I shall suggest you to get it checked by some legal advisor for the jargon, language and inclusion of all points.

- **Four Types of remuneration or fee**

Remuneration or fee of an interior designer is based on the service scope. You can categorize the fees in 4 different types.

1. You can do only consultancy and supervision for a particular project. Here, you can charge a per square

feet rate, lump sum or a certain percentage of total project cost ranging between 4-10% based on the scope of services and size of the project.

2. You can provide all your labours, carpenters, plumber, electrician, etc. You could form a good team and you can charge the labour fee plus a certain percentage of service charge ranging from 15-20%. This is a Labour Contract.

3. You can outsource all the purchases and the cost will be directly paid by theclient or to be reimbursed and as per the actual 5-10% of additional charges on the material can be your remuneration. This is a Material Contract.

4. You can do a total turnkey project based on the budget with a detailed estimate of the project. Here you need to quote the total project cost including your more or less profit margin of 15- 20%.

In real practice, a combination of these four can be worked out as per the client's requirement.

In addition to these the 3-Dimensional views or walkthrough animations are normally charged extra.

You can also include any additional site visits beyond the project schedule and outstation travel to source out the materials or furniture as extra per trip wise, local conveyance, flights, accommodation, food bills and per day remuneration.

- **How to make profit from your project**

Let me guide you that there are lots of hidden components in a specific item while doing Interior design. The client may see only the cost of material purchase and the cost of labour to apply the same. In reality, before you purchase any material, you need to select them and to do so you need to travel a lot or spend on your time and conveyance. This is known as material sourcing. Similarly, material cost also adds up to the loading, unloading and carrying cost. During application, materials are required to be fixed or applied with the help of adhesive, mortar, screw, nails, etc. this incurs some more cost in addition to the labour cost. Also to finish the product, you might require some finishing materials, Hardware, etc. To make it functional, you require some accessories. So these are the things which are beyond the knowledge of your client or a nontechnical person. And so these are the areas where you actually make the profit.

Please refer to the example of making a wardrobe/ cupboard as described in the estimation paragraph below.

- **Why and How to write a specification**

Here in this section, I am going to give you the super-easy method to write a specification. But before that, you should know why it is important to write a specification. Many of the practicing interior Designers briefly quote an item-wise summary to estimate the project. This is not the right method as this may create confusion regarding size, thickness, quality, make, finishing, etc. and conflict may arise with the client's expectation. Many designers follow a higher quote because of their lack of knowledge to write a proper description or specification so as to avoid later contingencies. Or many of them give this type of item-wise quotation without much description or specification for copyright purposes. Likewise, designer clients have also become very smart nowadays, they take the quotation from one and give the job to a different one. To safeguard yourself, you can also quote item-wise at the beginning and name it as a preliminary budget but do not provide a detailed estimate or BOQ (Bill Of Quantities). Once you get into an agreement with the client, you can produce a detailed estimate. Here, you need to describe all the items specifically. If you fail to describe or specify each detail of the item, you might be challenged later or at any time during the project or at the time of the final bill settlement. And there is a possibility to get your project omitted from your billed amount due to lack of clarity. So now you know why it is essential to write the specification and detailed description of an item and when.

Format to write a Specification

Now I would like to share that during our college days, I don't know why but our estimation specification class was the most boring one. Even now a lot of institutes either don't teach estimation specifications or teach in a wrong method enough to create hate rat among the students for the subject. Our professor in college used to come to the class every day with a big thick specification book and used to dictate the items one by one. A single item would start from the first line of a page and would be completed, maybe, at the end of the page or sometimes carry forwarded to the next few pages. Without understanding the inner detail we used to take the notes. And by the end of that semester, all of us used to have a big thick copy with too much description and specification without any knowledge to write a proper specification.

So later during my practice as an Architect Interior Designer and during my Institution lectures for my students, I have invented a very easy method to write a specification. I am sharing the same with you here.

Eight parts to include in a specification

One item description can have eight parts. The first part is the physical dimension and name of the items. 2nd the method of construction, 3rd the materials used to make the same and 4th the final or desirable finish, 5th how it can be achieved or method of application, 6th 7th and 8th are the smaller components within it. Now let us take an example. The cupboard below can be described as follows:

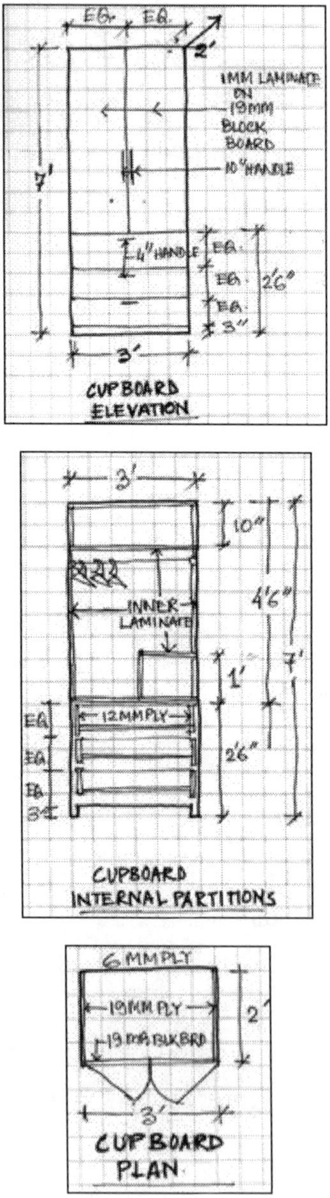
EQ. EQ.
2'
1MM LAMINATE ON 19MM BLOCK BOARD
10" HANDLE
7'
4" HANDLE
EQ.
EQ.
EQ.
2'6"
3"
3'
CUPBOARD ELEVATION
3'
10"
INNER-LAMINATE
4'6"
1'
7'
12MM PLY
2'6"
CUPBOARD INTERNAL PARTITIONS
6MM PLY
19MM PLY
19 MM BLKBRD
2'
3'
CUPBOARD PLAN

Fig. 1

Part 1: A cupboard having size 3' wide x7' High x 2' depth with two openable shutters above 2'6" and Three drawers in the bottom size of each to be mentioned as per the drawing.

Part 2: Here please note if the item follows a particular method then you need to mention it. In case of woodwork or so, you can mention the materials section insufficient to describe the item.

Part 3: Made of 19mm thick ply on both sides and shelves, two openable shutters made of 19mm blockboard, backside 6mm ply backing. Drawers are made of 12 mm ply sides and bottom, with 19mm blockboard facia.

Part 4: All finished with 1 mm selected laminate from all outside face and .72mm inner laminates from inside.

Part 5: Color: Here you need to describe all the color of the item visible from any side. Like inner laminates white or off white or something different outer laminates color.

Part 6: Texture: Matt, Satin, Glossy or anything to describe the touch and feel of the finish.

Part 7: Make: Why the make is important is because this guides the quality of materials, exact color and finished as visualized by the designer.

Part 8: Accessories: These include the hardware, fittings, any special mechanism/arrangements like slider/ Hydraulic/hinges, etc.

Once you are able to note down all your specification, it will look like this →

Providing and fixing 3'x2'x7' high Wooden cupboard, made of 19 mm block board openable shutter above 2'6" and Three drawers in the bottom size as per ID drawing, made of 19mm XXXX co. marine ply with 6mm ply backing, finished with .72 mm inner off white laminate of approved make from all inside surfaces and 1mm light xxxx color satin finish having code XXXX laminate of XXXX or similar company all external sides exposed to or visible from all sides. Also provide aaaa or similar company make modular accessories with zzzzz type of hinges, telescopic drawer channel, all necessary hardware, nails and screws all complete.

So now you know how to write a specification. Now you need to estimate the cost for the same. Based on the specification you have to calculate the estimated cost of the item. Let me show you how to do that. From the picture, it is very much clear what the materials are that you need to manufacture the cupboard. You need to make a list of the same as follows with the price and quantity.

		Qty	Unit	Rate	Amount
1	19 mm Ply for box structure and shelves	40	sq.ft.	152	6080
2	19mm block board for shutters	21	sq.ft.	148	3108
3	6mm ply backing	21	sq.ft.	80	1680
4	12mm ply for drawers (actual 27 sq.ft.)	32	sq.ft.	106	3392
5	.72 mm inner off white laminate (actual 90 sq. ft)	3	sheets	700	2100
6	1 mm outer selected laminate (actual 55 sq.ft.)	2	sheets	1900	3800
7	20" Hardware Drawer channels	3	pair	450	1350
8	Hardware Hinges	2	pair	220	440
9	Hardware Handle	5	nos	350	1750
10	Hardware (Latches, Magnet, Locks etc)	1	set	500	500
11	Fevical	10	kg	180	1800
12	Tapes, Nails screws	1	LS	2000	2000
13	Modular accessories	1	set	5000	5000
14	Carpenter	21	sq.ft.	350	7350
15	Material carrying cost	3	LS	700	2100
16	Material loading unloading	3	LS	350	1050
17	Edge banding or teak wood liping as per detail	100	rft.	50	5000
18	Misclleneous	1	LS	2000	2000
19	Drawing and supervision cost	1	LS	5000	5000
					55500

So now you know how to estimate the cost of furniture. You need to calculate the cost of each item like this then add. And do not forget to add contingency as 3-5% of the total budget, your remuneration and add all this to get your final quotation. It is very much important to be aware of the market price of each material, detailing out the item, specification and market competition too.

Once you are able to prepare your budget and get it approved by the client, you can get your first job. Now it is time to manage your first job smartly. In the next chapter, I am going to explain how you can handle your job carefully and successfully.

STEP 9

Manage Your Project

In this chapter let me make you understand the requirement of planning and managing projects in a proper method and with deep knowledge in various aspects of handling a project. Whether its a design consultancy or complete execution with or without material or any other type of project to understand different types of projects you need to read chapter 8. You need to be aware of the project life cycle, how it goes, what are the constraints you need to address, what are the different knowledge areas you need to plan, integrate, maintain throughout the life of a project. I shall also make you understand how different types of conflicts can be resolved once you are done with this chapter.

Here I will discuss the following:

- o Triple Constraint
- o Resourcefulness
- o 10 areas to give attention

Before we do so, we need to know certain terminologies.

Project: Anytime, anywhere anything can happen in a project. Project is an endeavor to accomplish a goal within a time frame and budget. As per PMBok (Project Management Body of Knowledge, PMI USA), a project is a

- ❋ ***Temporary endeavor***
  - ❋ Every project has a definite beginning and a definite end
  - ❋ Does not mean short duration
- ❋ ***Undertaken to create a unique product, service or result***
  - ❋ A product or artifact that is produced, is quantifiable and can be either an end item in itself or a component item
  - ❋ A capability to perform a service, such as business functions supporting productionor distribution
  - ❋ A result, such as outcomes or documents

❋ ***Progressive Elaboration***

❋ Developing in steps, and continuing in increments

And Project Management is the application of knowledge, skills, tools and techniques to project activities to meet the project requirements.

Project Life cycle:

Each and every project has its own start point and end point. Technically, it has five stages in the complete process. We initiate a project first with a brief description like will cook fried rice with Paneer. It comes from some need, want or desire. Then we start planning for the same. At the end of first level planning, we start executing the same. So we start the fieldwork. During the entire execution, it is obvious that we have to take control of our entire activities, budget, expenses, schedule, etc. Now during this stage, very often, we find certain changes that are required in our scope, schedule or budget. That time we need to go back and change our planning and execution accordingly until our goal is accomplished. Once our goal or target is achieved, most of us think the project is complete. However, this is not true. The project is complete only after handing over and completing all the billing, payments, settlements with each vendor and also completing the records and documentation. That is called closing. This is the complete project life cycle.

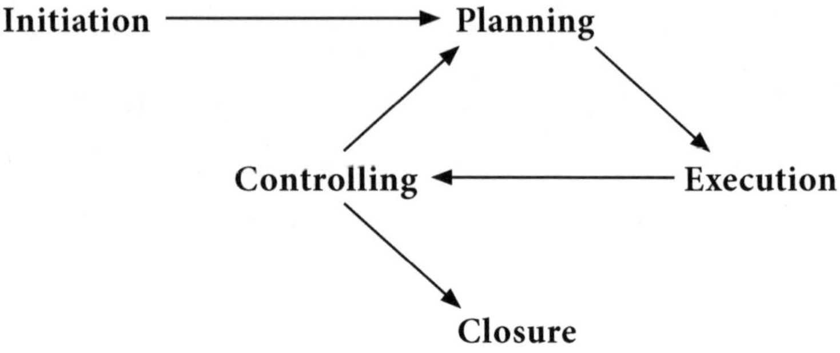

Project Life Cycle

Triple Constraints:

As a professional whether in creative design or any other industry, the main challenges lies in three major things.

- How much you need to deliver?
- Within what time frame you have to deliver?
- What shall be the cost of delivering the same?

These three components of your project are well defined and restricted, the so-called triple constraint for any kind of project. These are Scope, Time and Budget. The relationships between these three are predominantly affected by each other and result in the quality of the project.

Any project must have a defined scope without which the project cannot be started. Before you start a project, it is suggested that not only the scope for your client but you should have calculated and proposed the required time to completion and also a practical budget to complete. All these three are the preliminary guiding factor for your project. Till the project does not start, there is no or minimal risk of change in these three as we start only after getting approval from the client for all these parameters.

However, the problems start to seep in once the project starts. Due to various reasons, it is obvious to make changes in the request for any of these three parameters. Let me explain. By this time, you are able to handle small projects. Let's take an example of a modular kitchen. Let's review the scope for a kitchen with a size of, let's say, 10‘x6‘ with L- shape counter having a total length of 14‘. The start of the project may include having lower cabinets with modular accessories for 9‘ and a normal shelf with a ventilated shutter for 5‘. Similarly, having an upper head glass cabinet of 10‘ length with 2‘6” height covering the total length of the lengthier side of the kitchen. As per this defined and approved scope, you have calculated an approximate budget of, let's say 2.74 lacs with a time frame of 21days and have got the approval.

Now during execution, if your client‘s wife asks for more storage then you can't deny. So your scope added up with a loft above the upper head cabinet, i.e., scope has changed. Now it is obvious that you need more materials and labour. So it requires more budget and also longer duration to complete if you do not want to increase the number of carpenters because of space constraint. Here if your client agrees to increase both then all the three parameters would change. In another case, if the client keeps the time frame fixed for you and asks you to complete the additional work within the same time limit, you have to increase the number of labourers and hence, the budget increases. If the client freezes the budget for you that you need to complete the whole work with additional (variable scope) in the same budget and time, it will affect the quality of the work.

So you can easily understand that scope, time and cost (budget); these three are the major parameters where if any one or two changes, keeping the second and or third constant, it bears an effect on the work quality. So these three parameters are called triple constraints for a project Manager.

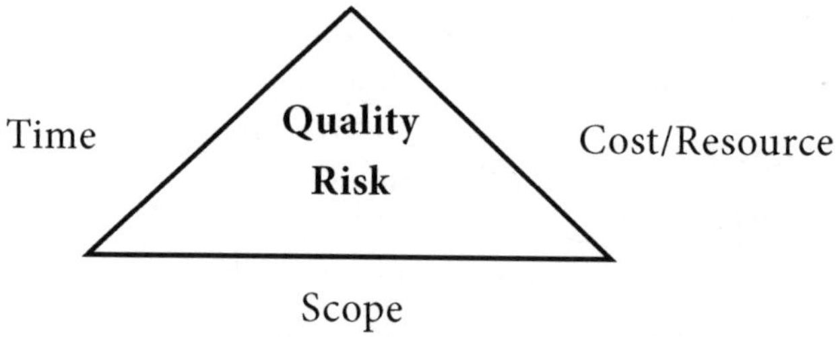

Tripple Constraints

Knowing the probable constraints beforehand helps to face and rectify. So it is very important to know how to handle Scope, Time and Cost; the triple constraint. Now to manage these, it is very important to be resourceful and knowledgeable. There are 10 different knowledge areas where constant monitoring helps in the successful completion of a project. Here, I have described all of them with more emphasis on the ones that are more important.

10 Knowledge Areas:

For our better understanding let us take an easy day-to-day example. If you are a responsible employee, you must be using your diary or pin-up board to keep notes about the work you need to do on a particular day in your office. We plan our holiday or weekend very carefully. The easiest example to understand the project knowledge areas is your mother's cooking or if you are a lady managing your family kitchen.

If you have to cook fried rice and paneer tomorrow, you check your refrigerator tonight to ensure if you have sufficient paneer, check your kitchen storage for other ingredients, check if the type of rice you have is suitable for fried rice or not, You gather all the ingredients for, maybe, Rs. 100, you plan the time to cook in the morning before you leave for your work, break those into parts like chopping, washing, preparation, cooking then serving time. Let's say, all the tasks take 1hr. You also plan for the availability of the fuel type, the utensils required for cooking and for keeping it hot and then serving.

Now you ask your maid to be present on the next morning without any fail. She charges Rs. 50 per day for cooking. You also keep an alternative plan if your maid does not come on time. Finally, in the morning you cook and serve hot.

This example might seem silly while reading but once I explain, you will be able to relate each of them one by one with the important aspects of a project.

- Plan for cooking Fried rice and Paneer is the project **scope**.
- Rs. 150 (Ingredients / Material + Manpower/work) is your cost of the project.
- 1hr. is your project **time**, scheduled for the next day morning.
- Purchasing materials and storing is your **procurement**
- Whether the maid comes or not is the **Risk** factor consideration.
- The type of rice checked is your **Quality** of the project.
- Your maid here is your human resource and ingredients are the material **Resources**.
- Your last night reminder call to your maid is **communication**.
- You, your maid, your family member who financed and who is going to relish the food are your **Stakeholders.**
- And last but not least, coordinating and maintaining the connectivity, organizing the whole thing is the project Integration.

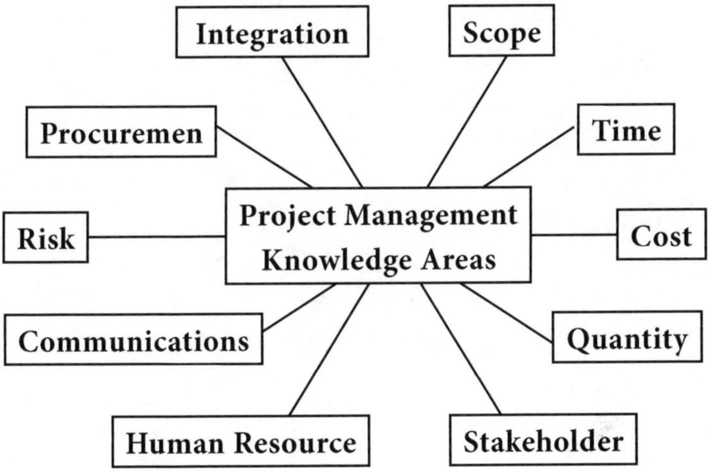

In one-liners:

1. The definition and description of the Job with detail deliverables is your scope.
2. The time needed to perform the whole job starting from initiation to handover and all payment closures from client to vendors is the time.
3. The total expenditure incurred during the project is cost.
4. Quality of a project is always directly proportionate to the scope, time and cost. Once any of these three area changes, the quality gets affected.
5. Starting from your client's each family, you, your design and execution team, labors, contractors, vendors, suppliers all are your stakeholders who can

affect your project or can be affected by changes in project scope, time or cost, if any.

6. Again the manpower who are directly working for this project whether design and supervision team or labors are your HR.

7. A clear, understandable communication between all thestakeholders should happen on time to maintain the project lifecycle.

8. It is recommended to list all the possible risks that might occur during the project lifecycle and one should list the possible remedies in advance.

9. All the materials need to be procured with a specific plan in advance.

10. Over and above, all these ten areas need to be coordinated throughout the project lifecycle. So now you understand the whole process in a simple platter.

While planning your project, you need to break down all your activities into the smallest or bottom- most possible activity level, so that you can assign minimum duration accurately to complete each activity. This is called **WBS** or work break down structure. After assigning the required duration for each activity if you simply connect all of them in a series you will have a project with the longest duration. So now you need to learn to build a relationship between various activities and plot them in a graph to get the least time duration to complete the project.

Most of your clients will not leverage the time and will ask you to complete their project as soon as possible. So it is very much important to know how to do this. Though this requires a thorough knowledge of **project scheduling** and can be best done with software like MS-Project or primavera, here I will recommend you to do the preliminary in even MS-excel or manually in a graph.

To do that let us understand the various possible relationships between different activities. Example: A Flooring labor can work for tile fixing in one room while the electrician can work in another room for electrical piping, at the same time plumber can work in the kitchen and toilet of the same house. By the time flooring is done in the living room the electrician can be shifted to the other room. In a similar manner, once plumbing work is done in the kitchen and toilet the flooring & wall tiling work can take place in the bathroom. Once the flooring is done in the living, dining and bedroom you should start the false ceiling work as soon as possible. All these types of activities are called parallel activities which can have a relationship of **start to start** i.e., can start simultaneously.

The relationship between the false ceiling framework and electrical piping is start to finish. Till the framing of false ceiling is not done electrical pipe layout for ceiling cannot be done. Or till the plumbing in toilet or kitchen is done the wall tile fixing cannot be done. All these are possible when one activity finishes then the other starts so **start to finish.** Most activities come under this relationship category.

The third category is **Finish to Finish**

Electrical wiring can start later than fixing frames and channels for the false ceiling at a site, but before you start fixing the ceiling board both electrical piping and framing should be completed. So you can put a finish to finish relationship for these two works and make the fixing of ceiling boards as a successor for both.

The fourth is **Finish to start**

This relationship is normal and common one. If task B can be started just after finishing task A, like the fitting of accessories in a modular kitchen, can be done after basic woodwork of ply boxing. Though these two activities are having a finish to start relationship yet the procurement of modular accessories are under start to start relationship with ply boxing or woodwork.

Now any of these relationships can have **lead or lag.** Let me explain. If Curing for concrete needs 7 day's time, though plastering can start after concreting of columns and beam can be done yet a lag of 7 days can be considered. So here plastering is having a relationship of finish to start with concreting with a lag of 7 days.

Lead: Lead is a term that you must be aware of. If two tasks are having a relationship of starting or finishing together but not exactly on the same date, where one task is starting after 3 to 4 days of the 1st task start date, it means task B is having a lead of 3 to 4 days. Or the task is lagging task A by 3 to 4 days.

Now to understand the different relationships, you can refer a manual gnat chart as given in the reporting system section below.

It is always necessary to follow and abide by the project schedule to control the cost of the project. Otherwise, in most cases, the project cost increases due to delay in the schedule. So you need to be very much careful about the timeframe of the project. Once you are able to plan the project and execute accordingly you can start making a good amount of profit.

Reporting System:

A major conclusion to managing projects can be drawn with the system of reporting and it's utility. By now you all know why we need to plan and control our project and how to do, where to focus, what are the knowledge areas need to be taken care of during any project. Now let me tell you that at regular intervals during project planning, execution and controlling reporting are also essential. In project planning and management, you can generate a number of different types of reports.

However, my primary focus in this book is to help you become an expert in managing your project without very deep knowledge or a degree but with the help of most important and essential practices.

Report type 1: Schedule of work with a specific start date and end date of each task is the first level report that needs to be generated and approved by the client even prior to the start of the project. If possible, you need to add a bar chart with the same for visual impact. This is an important aspect to show in this report:

2nd report that you need to get approved before starting the project is cash flow. Let's review how can you create this report. Let us assume you have estimated that the proposed tile work will take 2 weeks' time and 4 lakhs of Rupees. In the second week, you are also starting woodwork for one bedroom that requires Rs, 1 lakh and will continue for the next 2 weeks. In the third week, you have planned for the fixing of wallpapers that will take Rs. 20,000/- and 3 day's time. So, the cash flow for the first three weeks will be as follows:

	EC		WK1	WK2		WK3
Job 1	4L	+	2L			
Job 2	1L	+	50K	50K		
Job 3	EC			20K	+	20K
So, the cash flow =	2L		2.5L	70K	+	20K

This kind of report gives your client a clear idea about the flow or requirement of cash at any point in time for any week. So it is always a good practice to plan in advance. It also reduces any unplanned expectation on both fronts; you and the client.

The third report type that is necessary during the entire life cycle of the project is the progress report. Draw a 2nd bar along the 1st planned bar chart to show the actual start date and work done for a particular task. See the example below to understand.

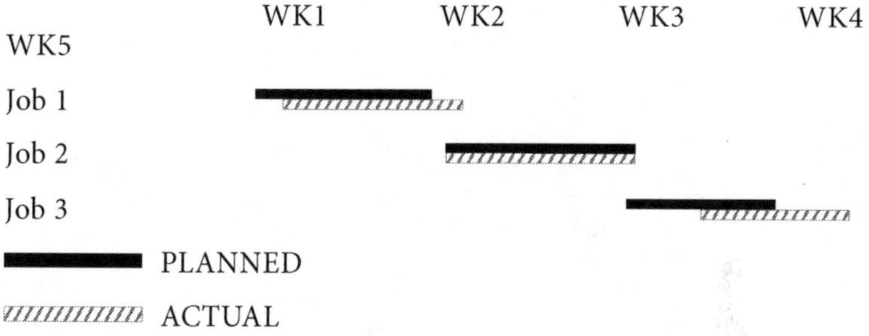

Here you can clearly explain to your client about the progress of the project. Job 2 started and finished on time here, whereas Job 1 and 3 are delayed and especially because of the delay in Job 3, the project end date gets delayed. You need to keep a record, document and inform the client about the cause of delay to avoid last-minute arguments.

You also need to communicate and document if there is any price change or change of scope. One more report is the to-do list. For your reference, you can keep a weekly to-do list ready. If helps minimize ship/miss in any job.

As a beginner, these reports are more than enough to keep a track of your project, to control triple constraints and manage the stakeholder effectively. To find more report types you may refer to any project management software like MS Projector or Primavera etc.

STEP 10

Successful Sales Leads To Abundance

This is the chapter that I like the most and I believe that once you go through the chapter, your inner ability to sell your design will enhance and you will also start liking the chapter the most. Most of the people start acquiring knowledge to start a business and they are very sincere in that. But in spite of being knowledgeable sometimes they fail because of their inability to sell their design. I will say, first sell yourself then sell your design.

- How to get my client
- How to satisfy them and satisfy own self too
- How to convince them about my design proposal
- How to keep a good relationship with my client throughout the project and after that also

- How to get references

So many other questions surface when it comes to the term 'successful sales'.

Here I want to refer to a famous book "MASTER THE ART OF SELLING" BY Tom Hopkins that is a best-seller but there is nothing written in it. All pages are blank. It actually implies that you will write the method or process through which you want to sell. If you look at all the questions I have listed above most have already been answered in the previous chapters. All you need to do is go back and check again.

The different kind of clients you meet during your professional career has been described in an earlier chapter.

1. The ideal way to get your first client as the best client is to approach through your friends, family members and people who trust you very much. Professionally, we will learn about accruing the client in a whole lot of processes at the end of this chapter.

2. To convince your client with your design, proposal and presentation matters a lot. Presenting your design with proper rendering has been described in Step 3 and 4.

3. Now maintaining a prosperous relationship with the clients and also satisfying them depends on three major things:

a. Aligning your services towards the scope.

b. Delivering on time and within budget. As a result of which quality matters.

c. Right communication that is verbal enough through visual reports etc. (this has been described in Step 9.)

4. Once you have satisfied your client and have maintained a good relationship, getting references is easier only if you ask for one. The process of eventuating satisfied clients with project details is very much important in the design profession. You need to create a good portfolio of your creativity with the feedback from the clients.

All these are the processes that you need to practice. The primary challenge lies in your ability to sell. I have met so many people in my life who say, I can't make a sale. There are many who want a job but they don't want to do a sales job. It is actually very funny because either they don't want to do a job or they don't know that every profession is based on sales only. When we try to get a project, we sell our old projects and experiences. When we meet our client for the first time, we sell our seller, when we visit the site for the first time, we sell our technical knowledge. After getting the project from preliminary concept to detailed drawing, we sell our Technical skill, knowledge and experiences. Over and above, throughout the project, we sell our confidence to the extent that we are rewarded with money. So the bottom line is that even after acquiring the required knowledge from this book, please engage yourself in lots of practices to sell your design, lose the deals, negotiate time, money, detailing, materials, everything.

8 Mantras to manage client effectively

Here I am giving you some mantras to become successful in managing clients.

1. Do not display your attitude inappropriately. The attitude of knowing everything or being knowledgeable than others, especially the client and being smarter than necessary to be should be avoided in any service industry. You need to work hard as well as work smart.

2. Stop using negative words while talking. Never say 'NO' directly on your client's face. Say, "Yes I can also try this way or use this material" or you can say, "My experiences say this could be a better option."

3. Be with your client during the site visit, material sourcing or general meeting. Always be with your client mentally and physically. If you show any kind of less interest during the discussion with your client, you may lose him. Always understand that projects, for you, may be a regular affair but for most of your clients it is the 1st time or only once in a lifetime experience, so let him feel good about your services.

4. Show limited options but pretend that you are ready to give as many options as possible. If you stick to only one alternative option, the client may think you are not giving enough of your time and attention. At the same time, 2-3 option gives them a feeling of getting more to choose from. Again, if you start giving 10 options, the client may be confused about selecting one. So help them select from minimum 2 and maximum 4 options.

5. Never ever lie to your client. Be honest. For the sake of profitability in the business, you might be selling things at a higher price. That is ok only when you are giving added quality and value to it. There is a possibility that the client might be aware of the market price of any materials/product or services. In case you add any product in your process of applying, estimating & wastage, carrying cost, labour or anything, do let the client know. In the case of services, differentiate the quality and value of the competition.

6. Never try to sell only your ideas. Find out the emotion attached to it from your client's side then suggest. The sale will happen automatically.

7. Give time to any conflict that arises during the project life cycle. Time heals everything. Try to be patient enough to listen to your client's complaint. Try to find out the root cause while moving on with the project and take the necessary action to solve the same. For

more than one problem, find a solution based on urgency and priority.

8. Last but not least, in case if you are unable to find out certain solutions, you should surrender and may ask for suggestions from seniors, vendors, suppliers and clients too. So you have to remove E from your **EGO**, **GO** straight forward and seek help. When we get stuck in something, we seek fresh ideas from others even if it is not enough technical to be adopted but it can give you a clue for a solution.

Now let me give you some tricks on how to gain your confidence while making sales.

To be more confident in your profession, you need 3 things:

- **The 1st one is Knowledge.** There is no other way to be confident about something if you are not knowledgeable enough. After you complete this book, get in the practice mode. This is your zone investment project after you finish this book. Yet I would suggest you to not to restrict yourself to this book only. Go for an in-depth online or offline course on Interior Design. You can go to our website and join our community where you can get all your questions answered by design experts. You can join our offline one-year course or online unlimited lifetime valid course. You may attend my webinars, watch my video tutorials, listen to all podcasts for small topics that are relevant to Interior Design Practice & Business tips. There is an ocean of learning with us. Learn! Learn! Learn! And Learn to boost your confidence.

- **The 2nd factor that accelerates your confidence level is Practice.** I have listed so many practices throughout this book. Besides, there are templates for your quick reference. Download all the necessary equipments from our website and start practicing. Take the online test at the end of all learning lessons. Once you become practiced enough, you become more confident.

- **Last but not least is be Quick-witted.** You must have the ability to say or do the right thing in an emergency. For this, you have to have knowledge of the subject as well as you need to practice. Being quick-witted comes only from practice. A lot of people do not involve themselves but observe and criticize. The better practice is to participate. It is not required to win over a discussion with your client all the time, but what is important is that you should participate, try to give an instant solution to a maximum number of problems. In case it is beyond your solving capability, you should consult. There are times when even if you are not 100% correct but your witty logics and confidence can result in a mutual agreement.

Knowing how to do successful sales is important all through the project process. To maintain balance throughout, you require to balance all the aspects of your life. These are some interpersonal skills that are the must skills.

Automation

CRM helps you in building References, which helps in magnetizing an abundant number of projects, thereby empowering you to earn in millions by transforming your creativity into your passion and your passion into your profession.

In addition to technical and sales skills, it is more important to know how to generate customer leads for your business. So the Digital Marketing knowledge has become essential anyway.

Once you have covered every single topic, in spite of being a non-technical person or from a non-engineering background, irrespective of Science, Arts or Commerce background, you will be able to become a successful entrepreneur in the field of creative design.

Let me now confess that the title of this book "Zero Investment Business" is actually not practical. Yes, if you understand that MONEY is the only thing that can be invested then the title is almost perfect for you. But in reality, you have already invested your precious time to learn the techniques. Now to get your first client, you need to invest or share your acquired knowledge with your friends and families. Once you get your first client, you need to invest your skills acquired through this book to impress them with your proposal. Before you start with the execution, make sure you consider mobilization of at least 20-30% of the total budget and then start. So you have started your business with absolutely ZERO Money investment.

Also, please note that in spite of the knowledge gained through this book but with no credential or certification might lead you to the backseat because of market competitions. Through this book, my objective has been to lead you to a Zero Investment pathway of earning. Now it is your responsibility to take it further. I would like to suggest to you the following:

- Get yourself registered at www.zeroinvestmentbusiness.com and start your business today.

- Go to our website www.onlineskills.profex.co.in and register for the mailer to get updates and give your feedback.

- Join our community at www.somaligsinha.com for associating with like-minded people.

- View, Like and Share our Facebook page SomaliGSinhaOfficial@fb, Instagram SomaliGSinha@ Instagram to get updates on new technologies and products.

- Subscribe to our YouTube channel SomaliGSinhaOnYoutube to listen and view more videos on this subject.

- Join our online or offline detailed, specific and result-oriented course on creative designs and learn continuously.
- You may opt for our consultancy support for your first one or two projects and get one-to-one learning session with me.
- Before you become more confident to start on your own, get some hands-on training yourself on all the 10 steps. Register at a discounted price at www.profex.co.in as a gift of completing level!
- Join our referral program to benefit others too.
- Join our community to get answers to all of your queries and meet like-minded people.

Made in the USA
Monee, IL
08 November 2026

67968598R00106